THE GREAT GATSBY

F. SCOTT FITZGERALD

NOTES BY JULIAN COWLEY

Longman

 York Press

The right of Julian Cowley to be identified as Author of this Work
has been asserted by her in accordance with the
Copyright, Designs and Patents Act 1988

YORK PRESS
322 Old Brompton Road, London SW5 9JH

PEARSON EDUCATION LIMITED
Edinburgh Gate, Harlow,
Essex CM20 2JE, United Kingdom
Associated companies, branches and representatives throughout the world

First published 1998
This new and fully revised edition first published 2004
Fourth impression 2006

10 9 8 7 6 5 4

ISBN-10: 0-582-82310-2
ISBN-13: 978-0-582-82310-5

Designed by Michelle Cannatella
Typeset by Pantek Arts Ltd, Maidstone, Kent
Produced by Pearson Education Asia Limited, Hong Kong

CONTENTS

PART FOUR
CRITICAL HISTORY

PART FIVE
BACKGROUND

PART ONE

INTRODUCTION

HOW TO STUDY A NOVEL

Studying on your own requires self-discipline and a carefully thought-out work plan in order to be effective.

- You will need to read the novel more than once. Start by reading it quickly for pleasure, then read it slowly and thoroughly.

- On your second reading make detailed notes on the plot, characters and themes of the novel. Further readings will generate new ideas and help you to memorise the details of the story.

- Some of the characters will develop as the plot unfolds. How do your responses towards them change during the course of the novel?

- Think about how the novel is narrated. From whose **point of view** are events described?

- A novel may or may not present events chronologically: the time scheme may be a key to its structure and organisation.

- What part do the settings play in the novel?

- Are words, images or incidents repeated so as to give the work a pattern? Do such patterns help you to understand the novel's themes?

- Identify what styles of language are used in the novel.

- What is the effect of the novel's ending? Is the action completed and closed, or left incomplete and open?

- Does the novel present a moral and just world?

- Cite exact sources for all quotations, whether from the text itself or from critical commentaries. Wherever possible find your own examples from the novel to back up your opinions.

- Always express your ideas in your own words.

These York Notes offer an introduction to *The Great Gatsby* and cannot substitute for close reading of the text and the study of secondary sources.

 CHECK THE BOOK

Michael McKeon's *Theory of the Novel: A Historical Approach* (Johns Hopkins University Press, 2000) is an excellent introduction to the history of the novel.

READING *THE GREAT GATSBY*

WHAT IS 'GREAT' ABOUT JAY GATSBY?

What is 'great' about Jay Gatsby? This question must surely arise in the course of any serious attempt to interpret F. Scott Fitzgerald's novel. *The Great Gatsby* was published in 1925, in the middle of a decade of hero-worship in America. Newspapers, reaching a larger readership than ever before, were extravagant in celebrating a feat such as Charles Lindbergh's solo flight across the Atlantic in 1927, while the careers of screen idols ranging from the romantic Rudolph Valentino to the comic Charlie Chaplin filled the pages of magazines eagerly purchased by Americans hungry for glamorous images.

 CHECK THE NET

http://www. founding.com offers a comprehensive account of the Founding Fathers and their Declaration of Independence that claimed to sever links with Old World ways and values.

But America, during the preceding century and a half, since its Declaration of Independence from Europe in 1776, had been fiercely proud of its identity as a modern democracy. In such a society, which boasted of the fundamental equality of all its citizens, the concept of greatness was far from straightforward. The Old World had its 'great' rulers: Alexander the Great, Peter the Great, Frederick the Great, Catherine the Great. In the United States, the epithet 'the great' was more likely to be attached to the name of some vaudeville magician or stage illusionist in a popular entertainment.

Jay Gatsby certainly defines himself according to European values, importing clothes and cars from England, living in a mansion based on a French model, and affecting the lifestyle of an Old World aristocrat. But his efforts do not convince; the traces of the boy from the American Midwest are evident through the veneer of sophistication, surfacing in moments of nervousness and uncertainty. He seems, then, to be closer to the New World version of 'greatness', 'The Great Gatsby' surrounded by props and assistants, conjuring magical effects which are almost, but not quite, believable.

In the same year that F. Scott Fitzgerald published this novel, John Dos Passos (1896–1970) published *Manhattan Transfer*, another book about New York, but a book without a hero. John Dos Passos creates a panorama of the city, moving from scene to scene, and from character to character, with no single event and no individual standing out significantly from the rest. In the 1920s America was becoming an urban society, its life was increasingly city-based, and that also complicates the notion of 'greatness'. Inhabitants of cities tend to become anonymous, to be drawn into the mass, and F. Scott Fitzgerald shared John Dos Passos's sense that America had become a culture of mass production and mass consumption.

In the urban, industrialised, standardised world of the twentieth century, heroic literary figures became more and more scarce. The individual achieving distinction through combat or quest or adventurous deeds had been largely displaced by the **anti-hero**, the passive victim, carried along on the tide of events, without control over his or her destiny.

In the early years of the twentieth century the diminished status of the hero was evident in works classed as **naturalism**, novels which showed their characters at the mercy of large and impersonal forces such as economics, heredity and disease. Such novels, which usually took the city as their location, painted a picture of the world as brutal and cruel. In America the main exponents of naturalism were Stephen Crane (1871–1900), Theodore Dreiser (1871–1945) and Frank Norris (1870–1902). F. Scott Fitzgerald read Theodore Dreiser in particular and his influence is evident in *The Beautiful and Damned* (1922), the novel which preceded *The Great Gatsby*.

After the gruelling experiences of the First World War, the anti-hero was often portrayed as a powerless figure, caught up in social processes that were rigidly mechanical, with no room to prove personal worth. The American writer Gertrude Stein (1874–1946) called this the 'Lost Generation', characterising an age which seemed to have no sense of historical purpose. It is depicted in the early novels of F. Scott Fitzgerald's friend Ernest Hemingway (1899–1961), such as *The Sun Also Rises* (1926) and *A Farewell to Arms* (1929), where the war is seen to be directly responsible for the impotence of the characters.

Gatsby's 'greatness', then, is a matter that demands our attention. Inescapably, it is caught up in the narration of his story, and that narration is entirely through the voice of Nick Carraway. It is Nick who makes Jay Gatsby into 'The Great Gatsby', and as we read we need to ask what kind of man this narrator is. Why is he so drawn

CHECK THE BOOK

Theodore Dreiser's best-known novel is *Sister Carrie* (1900). Stephen Crane's most powerful naturalist fiction is *Maggie: A Girl of the Streets* (1893). Frank Norris's *McTeague* (1899) is an especially memorable example of naturalist writing.

CHECK THE NET

http://www. geocities.com/ athens/olympus/ 1104/guide.html has a number of useful links to F. Scott Fitzgerald sites.

to the man who was his neighbour? What does this attraction reveal about his own character? Why should a studious worker in New York's financial sector decide to write a book about a man with shady underworld connections and unexplained wealth? What drives a solid Midwesterner, with apparently old-fashioned values, to write a lyrical account of a man tragically obsessed with a youthful love affair?

It is important to recognise that this is first and foremost a book about a man writing a book. The relationship of Nick to Gatsby established in this basic fact frames the presentation of all the other relationships between characters in the story. It should also enter into any consideration of the kind of book F. Scott Fitzgerald has written.

WHAT KIND OF BOOK IS *THE GREAT GATSBY*?

F. Scott Fitzgerald is renowned as the chronicler of the Jazz Age. In his short stories, in particular, he evokes not the pessimism and sense of powerlessness but the pleasure-seeking spirit of the decade following the First World War. The stories were written primarily to entertain, and few of them suggest that there is a Lost Generation concealed behind the veil of hedonism. Still, F. Scott Fitzgerald is adept at reflecting the character of the times. Contemporary commentators remarked that *The Great Gatsby*, a far more substantial literary achievement, captured the feel of 1922, the year in which it is set.

But the experience of reading the novel is very different to that of reading documentary description. *The Great Gatsby* is a short yet concentrated novel. As he began to write it, F. Scott Fitzgerald sent a letter to Maxwell Perkins (1884–1947), his editor at the publisher Scribner's, saying that he wanted his book to be extraordinary. He was aiming for beauty and simplicity, but at the same time he knew the book would be intricately patterned.

Its intricacy makes for richness, and it invites a range of interpretations. Few novels have attracted so much attention from literary critics. Maxwell Perkins commented when he first read the novel on the remarkable amount of meaning F. Scott Fitzgerald could get into a single sentence. The concentration of the prose does not, however, produce a book that is difficult or laborious to read.

On the contrary, as Maxwell Perkins noted, it seems in reading much shorter than it actually is, although it contains enough material to fill a book three times its length.

Its success can also be measured in terms of its popularity, the ready availability of several inexpensive paperback editions, and the fact that it has been adapted as a Hollywood movie on three occasions (in 1926, 1949 and 1974).

On the most straightforward level it can be read as a love story, the tale of a man's obsessive desire for the woman he has lost and the tragic consequences of that desire. On another level it is a social **satire**, mocking the follies of contemporary social life, the shallowness, hypocrisy and greed that F. Scott Fitzgerald recognised in America in the years following the First World War.

Another level was opened up by the American literary critic Lionel Trilling (1905–75) when he argued in 1945 that Jay Gatsby stands for America itself. It can be read as a meditation on the fate of American ideals in the modern world, a contemplation both of the vision that sustained early European settlement of the New World and the sacrifice of that vision to materialistic values in the course of the nation's rapid growth.

The novel raises the question of what makes a successful nation. Does the success of some in acquiring wealth necessarily disadvantage many others and so create a divided and failed society? In less tangible, but equally important, terms, does material prosperity necessarily lead to loss of valuable ideals such as honesty, loyalty and fairness?

That *The Great Gatsby* works so effectively across these levels is testimony to F. Scott Fitzgerald's technical resourcefulness and compositional skill. If he had portrayed Gatsby's longing for Daisy Fay in isolation, we would have a touching but ultimately trivial story, and it would probably seem a pathetic rather than a tragic tale. If it were just a reflection of social manners, or narrowly a satire upon the ways of the age, it might be an enlightening historical document, but it would have evident limitations as a work of literature. And if it were an abstract meditation on ideals, it might

CHECK THE FILM

The 1974 version starred Robert Redford as Gatsby and Mia Farrow as Daisy Buchanan. In 2000 an American TV movie version was made with Toby Stephens and Mira Sorvino in those roles. It is a beguiling story with enduring appeal as well as a major artistic achievement.

prove a diverting work of philosophy or sociology, but its appeal would be largely to specialised readers. To fuse these diverse aspects into a memorable work of fiction requires a particular array of techniques, stylistic devices and formal structuring.

CHECK THE BOOK

Keats's influence can be seen elsewhere in F. Scott Fitzgerald's work. Keats's 'Ode to a Nightingale' gave F. Scott Fitzgerald the title of his 1934 novel *Tender is the Night* ('tender is the night, / And haply the Queen-Moon is on her throne').

The prose is infused with a lyricism, which has resulted in numerous critics invoking the Romantic poet John Keats (1795–1821) as a presiding spirit in the book. Indeed, it has become common amongst critics to suggest that *The Great Gatsby* should be read as a poem is read, on account of its complex verbal and thematic patterning. Words and events recur in an elaborate web of cross-reference that indicates a degree of self-conscious artifice not found in works of **documentary realism**.

This is not to deny that element of historical accuracy which has already been noted, but rather to suggest that F. Scott Fitzgerald has produced a book that is an amalgam of realism and of **romance**. This term popularly suggests a love story, and F. Scott Fitzgerald's book is certainly that, but it has a more specialised sense defined by an earlier American writer, Nathaniel Hawthorne (1804–64). In 1850 Nathaniel Hawthorne published *The Scarlet Letter*, subtitled 'A Romance'. An introductory essay, called 'The Custom-House', includes this well-known description:

> Moonlight, in a familiar room, falling so white upon the carpet, and showing all its figures so distinctly, – making every object so minutely visible, yet so unlike a morning or noontide visibility, – is a medium the most suitable for a romance-writer to get acquainted with his illusive guests. There is the little domestic scenery of the well-known apartment; the chairs, with each its separate individuality; the centre-table, sustaining a work-basket, a volume or two, and an extinguished lamp; the sofa; the book-case; the picture on the wall; – all these details, so completely seen, are so spiritualised by the unusual light, that they seem to lose their actual substance, and become things of intellect. Nothing is too small or too trifling to undergo this change, and acquire dignity thereby. A child's shoe; the doll, seated in her little wicker carriage; the hobby-horse; – whatever, in a word, has been used or played with, during the day, is now invested with a quality of strangeness and remoteness, though still almost as

vividly present as by daylight. Thus, therefore, the floor of our familiar room has become a neutral territory, somewhere between the real world and fairy-land, where the Actual and the Imaginary may meet, and each imbue itself with the nature of the other.

I have quoted this passage at length because it captures so well the atmosphere of F. Scott Fitzgerald's novel, which shifts so often and with such dramatic effect from the glare of daylight into the glow of moonlight. *The Great Gatsby* renders the concrete world in striking detail, but (as in Hawthorne's summary) objects (such as the green light at the end of the Buchanans' dock, or the shirts that Gatsby displays with such pride) are imbued with some additional quality that escapes rational explanation.

F. Scott Fitzgerald's work seems far more modern than Hawthorne's romances from the mid nineteenth century. This is partly because he introduces the qualities of romance through the colouring granted to events by Nick Carraway. As Nick filters the elements of the story through his recollection, and through his self-consciously literary writing style, they take on layers of meaning which a documentary realist account could not produce. Yet the story remains credible because we accept that Nick is himself writing a book about Gatsby, a man who felt 'that the rock of the world was founded securely on a fairy's wing' (Chapter 6, p. 96).

This book might bear Gatsby's name, but we should not underestimate the extent to which its enduring qualities result from Nick Carraway's narration. He presents himself as the writer of the story, a man with literary leanings since his days at Yale, one of America's most prestigious universities. He is also a character in the novel, involved in the action. It is only through Nick that we know Gatsby; he is making him 'great' for us.

But how does his style of writing – condensed, lyrical, aesthetically self-conscious – match his picture of himself, the thirty-year-old bond dealer, with thinning hair and few opportunities for happiness or fulfilment? He talks in one breath of his mundane study of investments and securities, and in the next proclaims with romantic melancholy, 'At the enchanted metropolitan twilight I felt a

---

◉ CHECK THE FILM

In the 1974 film version of *The Great Gatsby*, starring Robert Redford as Gatsby and Mia Farrow as Daisy, director Jack Clayton frequently uses soft focus effects to suggest a transforming glow surrounding those two characters.

WHAT KIND OF BOOK IS THE GREAT GATSBY? continued

 CHECK THE FILM

The first film adaptation of *The Great Gatsby* was made in 1926, and was directed by Herbert Brenon and starred Warner Baxter as Gatsby.

haunting loneliness sometimes, and felt it in others' (Chapter 3, p. 57). How should we read his own amorous involvements, especially that with Jordan Baker, in the light of the radiance his storytelling casts upon the obsessive love of Jay Gatsby for Daisy Fay? Such tensions in our sense of Nick Carraway are amongst the most intriguing issues generated by the novel, and play a major role in its enduring success as a work of literature.

THE TEXT

NOTE ON THE TEXT

F. Scott Fitzgerald started work on *The Great Gatsby* in 1923, but it was in April 1924 that the serious writing of the novel began. At that time he wrote a letter to his editor, Maxwell Perkins, declaring that his new novel relied upon purely creative work, rather than the concoctions found in many of his stories, which he considered 'trashy'. His third novel would create a world that was both sincere and radiant. It required of him a sustained imaginative act. His approach was self-consciously artistic in a way his previous efforts had not been. Although he refers disparagingly to his stories, they did provide the financial means for him to spend time writing *The Great Gatsby*.

CHECK THE FILM
The second film adaptation of *The Great Gatsby* was directed by Elliott Nugent in 1949, and starred Alan Ladd as Gatsby and Betty Field as Daisy Buchanan.

The initial work was done in France, as the Fitzgeralds found the Riviera allowed them to live more cheaply than in New York. The typescript was sent to his publisher, Scribner's, in October 1924. Maxwell Perkins wrote in November, declaring it an extraordinary book, and suggesting changes. He felt Gatsby's past should be made less mysterious, and the source of his wealth more explicit. By the start of 1925 F. Scott Fitzgerald felt he had brought Gatsby satisfactorily to life.

F. Scott Fitzgerald, then living in Rome, made revisions to all nine chapters during proof-reading, and rewrote Chapters 6, 7 and 8. This rewriting shifted the account of Gatsby's life from the later chapters to Chapter 6.

He tried to secure serial publication in a magazine, in order to obtain additional payment, and to build up interest in the book. Magazine editors rejected it, primarily on the grounds that its subject matter, with its emphasis on adulterous relationships, might offend some readers.

A working title for the novel was *Among the Ash Heaps and Millionaires*, descriptive of the social inequality that provides a thematic focus for the story, but Maxwell Perkins considered it unsatisfactory. F. Scott Fitzgerald's own favoured title was *Trimalchio in West Egg*. Trimalchio was the host of lavish parties in the *Satyricon* by the Roman writer Petronius (*c*.27–66). Perhaps because its erudition signalled his serious intent in the novel, F. Scott Fitzgerald was very reluctant to abandon this title. Amongst others he considered were *On the Road to West Egg*, *Gold-Hatted Gatsby* and *The High Bouncing Lover*. The last two refer to the poem which serves as an epigraph to the novel. This verse, written by F. Scott Fitzgerald, is attributed to Thomas Parke D'Invilliers, a character in his first novel, *This Side of Paradise* (1920), based on his college friend John Peale Bishop (1892–1944).

CONTEXT

On 2 February 1926 a dramatised version of *The Great Gatsby* opened at the Ambassador Theater in New York.

At the beginning, before publication, F. Scott Fitzgerald requested a change of title to *Under the Red, White, and Blue*, but it was too late, and despite his evident reservations the book appeared as *The Great Gatsby* on 10 April 1925.

The text referred to in these Notes is the latest Penguin Classics edition, introduced by Tony Tanner.

SYNOPSIS

Nick Carraway, from the Midwest of the United States, writes an account of certain experiences which affected him deeply while he was working as a bondsman in the New York financial world. The key events centre upon the mysterious figure of his next-door neighbour, Jay Gatsby, who is renowned for his extravagant parties.

Nick visits Daisy Buchanan, a distant relative, and her husband, Tom, whom he had known at university. At their house he meets a young woman named Jordan Baker, and in time they develop a friendship, which is at times presented as a strangely subdued romantic attachment.

Tom introduces Nick to his mistress, Myrtle Wilson, whose husband, George, runs a garage in a bleak district on the outskirts of the city. At one of Gatsby's flamboyant parties, Nick learns from Jordan that Daisy and Gatsby were once in love. They were separated when Gatsby went to Europe, as a soldier, during the

First World War. Meanwhile, Daisy met and married the very wealthy Tom Buchanan. Five years after their brief love affair, Gatsby remains infatuated with Daisy. His parties are staged in the grounds of his ostentatious house in the hope that they will attract her attention, so he may win her back. In fact, their reunion occurs in a more intimate setting. At Gatsby's instigation, Nick invites Daisy to tea at his home, and there the former lovers meet again.

But Nick is disturbed by rumours which seek to account for Gatsby's concealed past. It becomes clear that Gatsby, who has changed his name from James Gatz, has become rich through shady dealings with underworld contacts. Gatsby's idealistic pursuit of Daisy is in sharp contrast to his other allegiance, to the memory of a ruthlessly opportunistic materialist named Dan Cody.

Gatsby's name appears to be linked to bootlegging, the illicit production and supply of alcohol, during a time when the consumption of such drink was prohibited in America. Tom challenges him with this accusation when the two meet. In response, Gatsby tries to get Daisy to declare her continued love for him, and to deny that she has ever loved her husband, but she is unable or unwilling to do so.

After a drinking party at the Plaza Hotel, Daisy and Gatsby drive back to their homes in his car. Myrtle Wilson, who has been arguing with George, her husband, sees the vehicle and mistakenly believes that Tom is driving it. She runs into the road and is killed. The car fails to stop. The body is found by Nick, Tom and Jordan, who are following in another vehicle. Later, Gatsby tells Nick that he intends to take the blame for the accident, even though Daisy was at the wheel. Next day, Gatsby is murdered in his pool by George Wilson, who then commits suicide.

Gatsby's funeral, in stark contrast to his parties, is virtually unattended, although his father arrives from the Midwest, proud of his son's achievements, which he believes resulted from a combination of natural ability, discipline and hard work.

Nick decides to return to the Midwest, where he is writing this story, but before leaving the city he encounters Tom, who admits he told George Wilson that Gatsby drove the car which killed Myrtle.

CONTEXT

Millionaires were increasingly visible in America towards the end of the nineteenth and beginning of the twentieth century. Figures such as John Pierpont Morgan (1837–1913), Andrew Carnegie (1835–1919) and John D. Rockefeller (1839–1937) amassed vast fortunes and acquired the status of legends in the popular press.

The novel ends with Nick contemplating Gatsby's house in the darkness, musing on the significance of Gatsby's dedication to a dream, and on the harsh reality which led to his destruction.

DETAILED SUMMARIES

CHAPTER 1

- Nick Carraway begins his narration, introducing himself and the novel's other major characters: Tom and Daisy Buchanan, Jordan Baker, and Nick's mysterious neighbour, Jay Gatsby.

Nick Carraway has returned to the Midwest, and is writing a book about events which occurred during a period he spent on the East Coast of America. He begins his narration with some self-analysis, trying to pin down pertinent aspects of his own character. He recalls his father's advice to show tolerance towards others, and to reserve judgement, adding that 'Reserving judgements is a matter of infinite hope' (p. 7).

Nick refers to Gatsby as 'the man who gives his name to this book' (p. 8), and he displays a certain **ambivalence** in his dedication to that man's memory. He is scornful of certain aspects of Gatsby's character and behaviour, but for others – his 'heightened sensitivity to the promises of life' and his 'extraordinary gift for hope' (p. 8) – he has unqualified admiration.

CONTEXT

For centuries the dukes of Buccleuch have been the major landowners in Midlothian, Scotland.

Nick says a little about his family, claiming descent from the dukes of Buccleuch, although his father runs the hardware business set up by his grandfather's brother at the time of the American Civil War (1861–5), in which he avoided service. Nick, on the other hand, was caught up in the First World War (1914–18), and that has caused considerable disruption in his life. On his return from Europe, he found that the Midwest, which was once 'the warm centre of the world', now seemed 'the ragged edge of the universe' (p. 9).

Moving to Long Island, New York, in 1922, Nick settles in West Egg, a suburban 'village' (p. 9). Nick's neighbour, Jay Gatsby, lives in a mansion. Generally, Nick finds himself living with 'the consoling proximity of millionaires', and in nearby East Egg there are 'white palaces' (p. 11).

Nick tells of a visit to the house of Tom Buchanan, an acquaintance from Yale University, and his wife, Daisy, Nick's second cousin once removed. Buchanan is physically powerful and extremely wealthy. Nick meets Daisy's friend Jordan Baker, who is a golfer.

Tom makes racist comments, drawing support for his views from a recently published book, Goddard's *The Rise of the Coloured Empires*. Jordan tells Nick that Tom is having an affair with 'some woman in New York' (p. 20). This mistress is responsible for a telephone call during dinner.

Later, in the moonlight, Nick catches his first glimpse of Gatsby, gazing as if transfixed by a green light at the end of the Buchanans' dock.

> **CONTEXT**
>
> The Professional Golfers' Association of America was established in 1916, and during the 1920s the golf tournament was a spectator sport drawing large crowds of onlookers.

COMMENTARY

Nick Carraway's narration takes the reader into his confidence; he is sharing with us the recollection of certain significant experiences. At the same time, it is clear that the act of telling is part of the process by which he comes to terms with those experiences and develops his understanding of them. Nevertheless, it is immediately noticeable that his style is challenging: his sentences can be grammatically complex, and his vocabulary is at times obscure. He establishes at the start that he is writing an account, and F. Scott Fitzgerald has attributed to him a certain amount of self-consciousness as a writer.

The self-analysis that begins the account should highlight for us the fact that Nick is a participant in the novel with his own specific characteristics. His narration is therefore not a neutral affair, and the information he offers us, together with the manner in which he presents it, is coloured by his character. In reading *The Great Gatsby* we need to be aware of what is being revealed about Nick, as well as of what he is disclosing about others.

Nick's allusion to his father's advice establishes the novel's larger concern with the relationship of the present to the past, and with what is transmitted from one generation to another. This clearly has relevance to Gatsby's personal history, his rejection of his parents and his association with Dan Cody, his 'mentor', but it is also relevant to the history of America, which broke away from the paternal rule of European monarchy and declared itself a new country, free from the constraints of the past. This American commitment to the future, where anything might happen, is also suggested in Nick's reflection on reserving judgement as a matter of 'infinite hope' (p. 7). The national faith that it is never too late to start afresh persists. Note that it is Gatsby's 'extraordinary gift for hope' (p. 8) that ultimately draws Nick to him.

The new beginning has long been associated in the American mind with movement westward. After moving East in order to seek material success, Nick has now returned to the Midwest, to the heart of America, where he is able to pause and reflect upon the past few years. Nick declares, with **irony**, that in going East he 'was a guide, a pathfinder, an original settler' (p. 9).

CONTEXT

The American novelist Henry James (1843–1916), who spent much of his life in Europe and eventually settled in Rye, a Sussex coastal town, had already made this tension between European prestige and American money the predominant theme of his fiction, from relatively simple early novels such as *The American* (1877) through to complex late ones such as *The Ambassadors* (1903).

Significantly, Nick and Gatsby both reside in the New York suburb of West Egg. It is less fashionable than nearby East Egg, and its name carries with it connotations of the westward movement that characterised America's Frontier past (see **The Frontier** in **Themes**). The suggestion is that both Nick and Gatsby preserve American ideals which have been lost in the sophisticated cities of the East (see **American ideals** in **Themes**). This is, of course, ironic, as both Eggs are located on the East Coast. Further irony arises from the name 'Eggs'; they seem to promise new life, while in fact they are sterile rocks.

The purported romantic descent of the Carraways from the British aristocracy is in stark contrast to the far from glamorous material reality of a family hardware business selling goods of a highly practical kind. F. Scott Fitzgerald is developing the novel's thematic concern with the relationship between the New World and the Old, European prestige and American money. In *The Great Gatsby*, importations from Europe are an index of social status; much is made, for example, of Gatsby's Oxford education, his Rolls-Royce car, his mansion based on a French model, and his shirts sent from London. These items help to construct an image, but in the American context the image is a sham, a mere pretence.

Reference to his great-uncle avoiding participation in the American Civil War and finding success in business contrasts with the participation of both Nick and Gatsby in the First World War in Europe. It is stressed that Gatsby's military career was one of the keys to his social advancement. The continuing involvement of America in armed conflict signals the failure of an early American ideal, the aspiration to be a peaceful nation.

It should be noted that although the First World War ended in 1918, Nick's move to the East did not occur until 1922. This may confirm our sense that he is not an impetuous person, but it might also suggest that it was not just the war that unsettled him. Possibly his failed love affair back home played a larger part in his decision than is explicit in his comments. Nick does not present himself as an emotional or passionate man, but then his imaginative writing style does not seem to correspond to the outlook of a matter-of-fact worker in finance. Careful reading may lead us to conclude that there are emotional depths to Nick's character that do not feature in his own self-portrayal. Perhaps there are sensitivities and vulnerabilities that he chooses not to disclose or is unable to confront.

The Buchanans have spent a year in France, not (like Gatsby and Nick) on war service, but in pursuit of pleasure. F. Scott Fitzgerald describes them as wealthy drifters. Their casual, aimless way of life establishes the terms for a sharp and telling contrast with the schedule of self-discipline drawn up by young James Gatz and displayed with pride by his father following Gatsby's death (Chapter 9, p. 164).

The ringing of a telephone is just one indicator that this is a twentieth-century technological environment, the world of cinema, cars, motor boats, hydroplanes and gramophones. We recognise through such details that the 1920s was a decade of mass media, mass production and mass consumption in America. The novel raises the issue of individual worth within such a context (see **Historical background**).

CONTEXT

Ernest Hemingway's novel *The Sun Also Rises* (1926) is the classic account of uprooted Americans drifting aimlessly in Europe in the aftermath of the First World War. Such figures came to be known as the Lost Generation.

In contrast to the artificial world of manufactured goods, Daisy's name evokes a delicate white flower. The irony here is that her life is conducted in an entirely manufactured environment, remote from the natural world. A little later, Nick remarks that Daisy opens up 'in a flower-like way' (p. 24), but her artificiality makes this simile as unconvincing as when Daisy compares Nick to a rose (p. 19). Myrtle, whom we meet in the next chapter, also has a plant's name, although the myrtle is a dark, hardy shrub. The plant seems to suit her character, and her environment, and the fact that myrtle was considered in the ancient world to be sacred to Venus, the goddess of love, is ironically appropriate to her role as Tom's mistress.

It should be noted too that Carraway, spelt 'caraway', is the name of a tall, yellowish plant with thin leaves. Its seeds are widely used in cooking. Does this detail tell us anything about Nick? The homely name Carraway certainly seems distant from the upper-class name of the dukes of Buccleuch, to whom, Nick suggests, his family may be related. Buchanan, on the other hand, is actually the name of a Scottish clan with territory near Loch Lomond, in Stirlingshire. Tom Buchanan belongs very evidently to an American upper class whose privileges are based in wealth.

Tom Buchanan's racist comments reveal an American reality of social division by race as well as by class and by gender. The United States has a Latin motto: *e pluribus unum*, meaning 'one from many'. It was chosen in 1776, at the founding of the republic, and indicated that thirteen separate colonies were combining to form a single nation. With hindsight we can see that this phrase has deepened in significance as the population of America has grown through consecutive waves of immigration, refugees or voluntary emigrants from other countries seeking a fresh start in the New World. The motto now suggests that these diverse newcomers have blended into a unified social fabric, often referred to as a 'melting pot'.

American history shows that in reality intense rivalry and conflict have often existed between groups with different cultural backgrounds, striving to succeed in an intensely competitive environment. Tom Buchanan considers his own northern European

CONTEXT

The term 'melting pot', signifying America's assimilation of immigrants from diverse backgrounds, was taken from the title of a 1908 play by Israel Zangwill (1864–1926), an English Jewish writer. Zangwill argued that in America all the races of Europe were melting and re-forming like different metals blending in a crucible.

ancestry to be a sure indication of his social superiority to members of groups with other backgrounds, especially African-Americans, many of whose antecedents were taken forcibly to the New World as slaves.

CHECK THE BOOK

Maldwyn A. Jones's *American Immigration* (University of Chicago Press, 1992) is a readable and authoritative study of the complex role played by immigration in the formation of American identity.

GLOSSARY

8   **the Civil War** America was torn by traumatic conflict between the Northern and Southern states between 1861 and 1865. The abolition of slavery was a major positive outcome, but many of the nation's cherished aspirations were severely damaged by the war

9   **New Haven** town in Connecticut where Yale University is situated

10   **Midas and Morgan and Maecenas** Midas was a legendary king of Phrygia, whose wish that whatever he touched turned to gold was granted by the god Dionysus. He soon recognised that this apparent blessing was in fact a curse. John Pierpont Morgan (1837–1913) was an extremely wealthy American financier, who spent large sums in building an art collection. Gaius Maecenas (c.70–8BC) was a Roman diplomat and friend of the Emperor Augustus. His name has become synonymous with generous patronage of the arts

    the egg in the Columbus story it was suggested to Christopher Columbus (1451–1506) that another explorer would have discovered America, if he had not. In response, he issued a challenge to make an egg stand upright. Only he, by flattening one end, succeeded. It was possible for others but he found the way

11   **one of the most powerful ends** an 'end', in American football, is the player at the end of the line, facing the opposition, required to be a good sprinter

    Lake Forest northern suburb of Chicago, inhabited by the wealthy

12   **Georgian Colonial mansion** an eighteenth-century building. The description recalls the revolutionary origin of the United States, which in 1776 broke away from colonial rule by the Hanoverian kings continued

---

CHECK THE NET

For more on the Georgian Colonial style visit **http://www. designintuit.com/ issue0002/focus/ ghistory.html**

CHECK THE NET

For more on the White Star Line visit **http://home. pacbell.net/steamer /wspage.htm**

GLOSSARY

18 ***The Rise of the Coloured Empires* by this man Goddard** apparently an allusion by F. Scott Fitzgerald to Lothrop Stoddard's *The Rising Tide of Color Against White World Supremacy*, published in 1920

20 **a nightingale come over on the Cunard or White Star Line** the bird immortalised by Keats in his Romantic ode is not found in America, so Daisy imagines one to have travelled the Atlantic on a British ocean liner

22 ***Saturday Evening Post*** a widely read magazine, to which F. Scott Fitzgerald was a regular and well-paid contributor

23 **Westchester** an exclusive northern suburb of New York City

Asheville and Hot Springs and Palm Beach fashionable resorts in Northern Carolina, Arkansas and Florida respectively

24 **Louisville** a town in Kentucky, in the American South

CONTEXT

The affluent side of 1920s America was highly visible through the new and expanding media. In 1929, however, the Wall Street Crash, in which the values of stock market shares plummeted, heralded the Great Depression, an economic catastrophe which blighted the lives of many Americans throughout the 1930s. Vulnerable citizens like the Wilsons were soon to be plunged far deeper into poverty and hardship.

Chapter 2

- Tom introduces Nick to his mistress, Myrtle Wilson.
- They go to an apartment in New York, where a small party takes place, involving Myrtle's sister Catherine, a photographer named McKee and his wife.

Nick describes the 'valley of ashes' (p. 26), a desolate area between West Egg and New York City, presided over by the huge bespectacled eyes of Doctor T. J. Eckleburg, an advertising hoarding erected by an optician. It is here that he is introduced to Tom's mistress, Myrtle, who is married to George Wilson, a car mechanic who runs a garage in this run-down spot.

Myrtle accompanies Tom and Nick into the city, where she buys (amongst other consumer items) cosmetics, magazines and a dog.

They go to an apartment kept specially for Tom and Myrtle's adulterous liaison. They are joined by her sister Catherine, a photographer named McKee and his wife, and a party takes place. Nick gradually gets drunk. Catherine mentions the cloud of speculation surrounding Gatsby, notably that he is a relation of Kaiser Wilhelm, the ruler of Germany during the First World War.

Tom breaks Myrtle's nose, in response to her defiant repetition of Daisy's name. Nick leaves with McKee, who, childlike in his drunkenness, takes to his bed and shows Nick his photographs. The chapter ends with Nick in Pennsylvania Station, awaiting the 4 a.m. train home.

COMMENTARY

The description of the 'valley of ashes' (p. 26) recalls the bleak spiritual landscape of T. S. Eliot's poem *The Waste Land*, published in 1922, the year in which *The Great Gatsby* is set. That poem responds to the horrific violence of the First World War but also to the spread of materialistic, consumerist values in modern society. T. S. Eliot (1888–1965) was an American, born in St Louis, Missouri, but he became a high-profile expatriate, settling in London and becoming eventually a confirmed monarchist and member of the Anglican Church.

Nick Carraway is writing his book in the Midwest, the heart of America, and near the end he declares it to be a tale of the West. Fitzgerald wanted *The Great Gatsby* to be a distinctively American novel. At the same time he felt it necessary to show the complicated relationship of New World ideals to Old World values. The novel is enriched by Fitzgerald's **ironic** treatment of that relationship.

Doctor Eckleburg's advertising hoarding is a realistic detail from the consumer culture of the 1920s. A visual advertisement of this kind had the additional merit of being comprehensible to newly arrived immigrants with little or no grasp of English. On another level, the eyes provide a striking focal point for the book's thematic concern with vision. The hoarding assumes potent significance at the end of the novel, when George Wilson mistakes the eyes for those of an omniscient God. Fitzgerald seems to suggest that consumerism and materialism have taken the place of spiritual values in modern America and have become pervasive.

CONTEXT

Kaiser Wilhelm II of Germany had some eminent relatives, notably amongst the British monarchy. Queen Victoria was his grandmother, Edward VII his uncle and George V his cousin. Despite this the two countries engaged in momentous warfare between 1914 and 1918, and it was into this conflict between closely linked monarchies that America was eventually drawn, despite its aspiration to remain distant from Old World discord.

CHECK THE BOOK

Susan Strasser's book *Satisfaction Guaranteed: The Making of the American Mass Market* (Pantheon, 1989) expands upon this point.

CONTEXT

The novel *Elmer Gantry* (1927) by Sinclair Lewis (1885–1951) is a scathing depiction of evangelical religion's techniques of persuasion being applied to cynical and thoroughly materialistic ends in modern America.

The Wilsons live at their place of work. This indicates that they have lower social standing than Nick Carraway, who works in the city but lives in a suburb, at a distance from work. The very rich in this novel seem not to work at all, and can live where they choose. F. Scott Fitzgerald is emphasising that America, despite claims to democratic equality, is a society divided into a number of social classes based on wealth and property. F. Scott Fitzgerald was attracted to the lavish lifestyle of the wealthy, yet he was also impressed by the political and economic analysis of capitalist society made by Karl Marx (1818–83) and had a keen sense of social injustice in twentieth-century America.

We see Myrtle buying various items, but should recognise that in turn she is, in a sense, being bought by Tom Buchanan. He buys her gifts, including a dog as a pet, but Tom views his relationship to Myrtle in material terms, as a physical affair rather than an emotional commitment. The relationship stands in stark contrast to Gatsby's idealistic devotion to Daisy.

This chapter is a brilliant cameo of a drinking party, and F. Scott Fitzgerald renders the increasing drunkenness of the company with great skill through understatement. He avoids the large and clumsy gestures suggested by intoxication, but includes a splendid moment where Nick, his reserve broken down by alcohol, wipes shaving cream from McKee's face. It should be remembered that this drunken scene is set against the backdrop of Prohibition in the United States (see **Historical background**).

CONTEXT

A National Prohibition Act was passed in the United States in 1919 and remained in force until 1933. It placed severe limitations upon the production and consumption of alcoholic drinks. It is hinted in this novel that Gatsby's wealth is due, in part at least, to his involvement with bootlegging, the illicit supply of alcohol.

GLOSSARY	
26	**borough of Queens** the swamp at Flushing Meadows, in Queens, was used in the 1920s as a site for the disposal of ashes from domestic heating. This was the factual basis for F. Scott Fitzgerald's 'valley of ashes' (p. 26)
30	**John D. Rockefeller** (1839–1937) famous oil tycoon
31	**ladies swinging in the gardens of Versailles** a reference to the famous picture *The Swing* (1766) by Jean Honoré Fragonard. Versailles was the magnificent palace of the French king, Louis XIV, and symbolised his absolute power as monarch

> **GLOSSARY**
>
> 31   **Simon Called Peter** this novel by Robert Keable was a bestseller in 1922. It tells the story of a young clergyman, whose experiences as a chaplain during the First World War resulted in loss of religious faith
>
>   **Broadway** a street in New York, renowned as the city's centre for theatre

CHAPTER 3

- A larger party is staged at Gatsby's mansion.
- Nick meets Jordan there. He notes that lurid speculation concerning Gatsby's past is rife, and then he has his first meeting with the man himself.
- The evening ends with a car accident outside the big house.

Nick describes Gatsby's opulent and ostentatious lifestyle. He owns a yellow station wagon and a Rolls-Royce. He also employs servants to maintain the neat appearance of his property, and to rectify any damage caused during his riotous parties.

At a party, Nick meets again with Jordan Baker, who has recently lost in a golf tournament. The cloud of 'romantic speculation' (p. 46) surrounding Gatsby becomes thicker as the gossip intensifies; it is said, for example, that he killed a man, and that he was a spy in the war (p. 45).

Nick encounters a man wearing owl-eyed spectacles in Gatsby's 'high Gothic library' (p. 46). The owl-eyed man, who has been 'drunk for about a week' (p. 47), is impressed by the room's authenticity, especially the fact that it contains real books (p. 47).

Then, for the first time, Nick meets his host, although initially he does not realise that it is Gatsby. Gatsby claims to recognise Nick from the war, and they share memories of 'wet, grey little villages in France' (p. 48). Gatsby uses the Anglophile term 'old sport', which he affects throughout. Nick notes that Gatsby has 'one of those rare

> **CONTEXT**
>
> Gothic was the name given to the dominant style of architecture in western Europe during the Middle Ages. Gatsby's library is, of course, a revival of that old style, an imitation. A Neo-Gothic fusion of Gothic trappings and modern design flourished in America between the turn of the twentieth century and around 1930. A notable instance in New York City's Manhattan district is the Woolworth Building (1913), known during the 1920s as the Cathedral of Commerce.

CHECK THE NET
Examples of genuine High Gothic architecture can be found at http://www.bc.edu/bc_org/avp/cas/fnart/arch/high_gothic.html

QUESTION
What do you think 'the most amazing thing' revealed by Gatsby might be?

smiles with a quality of eternal reassurance in it' (p. 49). But he also perceives a rough reality beneath his cultivated charm and even a risk of absurdity in the precariousness of his image.

Gatsby receives telephone calls from Chicago and Philadelphia in the early hours of the morning, suggesting underworld business connections. Nick is puzzled and intrigued. He comments that 'young men didn't – at least in my provincial inexperience I believed they didn't – drift coolly out of nowhere and buy a palace on Long Island Sound' (p. 50). Gatsby speaks privately with Jordan. She tantalisingly hints that he has disclosed 'the most amazing thing' (p. 53).

On leaving, Nick witnesses 'a bizarre and tumultuous scene' resulting from a car accident (p. 54). Then the chapter concludes with Nick's comments on what he has written so far. He remarks that the events forming the story absorbed him infinitely less than his personal affairs – work, study of investments and securities, and a short love affair that faded away. He admits to feeling 'a sort of tender curiosity' (p. 58) towards Jordan.

He remembers a news report (approaching scandal) concerning Jordan cheating at golf, and concludes, 'She was incurably dishonest' (p. 58). In the discussion that follows, Jordan says, 'It takes two to make an accident' (p. 59). Then she adds, 'I hate careless people. That's why I like you.' Nick confides that 'for a moment I thought I loved her. But I am slow-thinking and full of interior rules that act as brakes on my desires'. He concludes, 'I am one of the few honest people that I have ever known' (p. 59).

COMMENTARY

Gatsby's lifestyle is an obvious example of 'conspicuous consumption' (see **Historical background**). This extends to both of his cars, which stand out from the majority of vehicles on the streets. Henry Ford (1863–1947), who pioneered motor manufacture in the United States, promoted his automobiles as symbols of democracy. Ford cars were cheaply produced and most Americans could afford one. But Gatsby could not be satisfied with a standard black box, and the very showiness of his vehicles, intended to impress Daisy, plays a crucial part in his downfall. They are easily recognised, and following Myrtle Wilson's death in Chapter 7 it is easy for her husband to track down the owner.

Ford was, of course, by no means the only American producer of automobiles in the early twentieth century. Edward S. Jordan commenced manufacture of cars in 1915; the Baker Company made vehicles powered by electricity between 1899 and 1915. It is surely no coincidence that the name of the decidedly modern and mobile Jordan Baker combines the names of two makes of car. Once again, with Gatsby's Rolls-Royce, we see importation of the trappings of privilege from class-stratified Europe to supposedly egalitarian America.

The Gothic style of Gatsby's library harks back to European models, but this Old World echo was very much in vogue in America at the time that *The Great Gatsby* was written. The owl-eyed man appreciates the room, but he sees it through an alcoholic haze. His week-long drunken binge has taken place despite the restrictions upon production and consumption of alcohol during America's era of Prohibition. Gatsby's wealth, it has been heavily implied, is largely derived from illicit sale of alcohol.

We are told that the invitation Gatsby sends to Nick is signed 'in a majestic hand' (p. 43). In the artificial world of his parties, Gatsby watches events with the dignified detachment of an Old World monarch. Yet his guests conduct themselves 'according to the rules of behaviour associated with an amusement park' (p. 43). These people form a social elite, yet their behaviour is characterised in terms of vulgarity: another instance of disparity in the novel between pretension and reality. Amusement parks were very much a feature of New York life in the 1920s (see **Historical background**).

The speculation about Gatsby's past is an extreme case of a larger thematic concern in *The Great Gatsby* with reconstruction of past events. It is evident from the novel that recollection is inextricably linked to **point of view**. So, the past may exist in different versions according to whose memory is involved. This thematic issue is clearly linked closely to the narrative technique employed by F. Scott Fitzgerald, where the version of events we receive is exclusively that constructed by Nick Carraway.

CONTEXT

The term 'conspicuous consumption' was used by the American sociologist Thorstein Veblen (1857–1929) in *The Theory of the Leisure Class: A Study of Economic Institutions* (1899) to identify the tendency of the rich to display their wealth through extravagant purchases.

CONTEXT

The engineer Henry Royce (1863–1933) and aristocratic entrepreneur Charles Rolls (1877–1910) first met in Manchester in 1904. Later that year they began in partnership to produce cars of superior quality for an elite class of drivers. The name Rolls-Royce was linked from the start with social prestige.

GLOSSARY

42   **Castile** a province in central Spain

      Gilda Gray's understudy Gilda Gray (1901–59), who changed her name from Marianne Michalski, came from a Polish immigrant family, and sang in Midwestern bars before being discovered by the impresario Florenz Ziegfeld (1869–1932). She was the highly paid star of his 1922 *Follies* and was best known for her scandalously suggestive 'shimmy' dance

47   **Volume One of the *Stoddard Lectures*** John L. Stoddard (1850–1931) was the author of numerous travel books

      Belasco David Belasco (1853–1931) was an American dramatist and theatre manager, founder of the Belasco Theater in New York, who gained notoriety for the extravagance of his production methods, in the service of greater realism on stage

---

CHAPTER 4

- Gatsby visits Nick's house for the first time, and talks of his wartime experiences.
- They travel into the city, where Gatsby introduces Nick to Meyer Wolfshiem.
- Later, Jordan tells Nick about Daisy's past, her brief love affair with Gatsby, and her subsequent marriage to Tom.

Nick lists visitors to Gatsby's house, indicating the composition of his social set. Gatsby visits Nick for the first time and Nick notes the restlessness 'continually breaking through his punctilious manner' (pp. 62–3). Gatsby tells of his Midwestern upbringing, his Oxford education, his war service and the act of bravery which led to his promotion to the rank of major. Nick senses he is not telling the truth, although a photograph from Oxford and a medal awarded in Montenegro seem to confirm certain aspects of his account. Gatsby alludes enigmatically to the sad thing that happened to him.

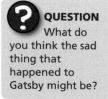

QUESTION
What do you think the sad thing that happened to Gatsby might be?

Over lunch, in New York City, Gatsby introduces Nick to Meyer Wolfshiem, who recalls the murder of his friend Rosy Rosenthal at the Metropole Hotel. Soon afterwards Gatsby discloses that Wolfshiem is a gambler, who fixed the 1919 World Series baseball tournament.

Then Nick introduces Gatsby to Tom Buchanan. Gatsby departs suddenly, evidently embarrassed. The narrative cuts to that afternoon, when Jordan is talking to Nick about the occasion in 1917 when she saw Daisy with a young lieutenant who was, it transpires, Jay Gatsby. The soldier was sent overseas, and was promoted to the rank of major, and Daisy married a rich man. This set of circumstances created Gatsby's current dilemma.

Jordan was a bridesmaid at the Buchanans' wedding, which was a notable social event. She tells how she found Daisy, prior to the bridal dinner on the day before her wedding, drunk and clutching a letter, obviously sent by Gatsby. Soon after their marriage, Daisy became pregnant, and Tom became an adulterer.

Nick comes to an understanding of the nature of his neighbour's desire and his obsessive love. Jordan conveys Gatsby's request to be invited to Nick's house when Daisy is present. The chapter ends with Nick embracing and kissing Jordan.

CONTEXT

In 1919 the Chicago White Sox baseball team succumbed to bribery and contrived to allow the Cincinnati Reds to win the World Series tournament. This was one of America's greatest sporting scandals. Arnold Rothstein (1882–1928), the real-life model for Meyer Wolfshiem, provided most of the money required to fix the result.

COMMENTARY

The list of guests who visit Gatsby's party is a comic set piece, a literary exercise, which includes puns and verbal jokes. It is quite distinct from the lyrical prose in which much of the novel is written, and seems more in keeping with a novel of manners such as William Thackeray's *Vanity Fair* (1847–8), which F. Scott Fitzgerald admired, and which contains similar lists.

Note that there are plant names here: 'Hornbeam', 'Endive', 'Orchid', 'Duckweed'; animal names: 'Civet', 'Blackbuck', 'Beaver', 'Ferret', 'Klipspringer'; and names of sea creatures: 'Whitebait', 'Hammerhead', 'Beluga'. Should we read these names as a satirical ploy, suggesting certain characteristics associated with these natural phenomena that are shared by the characters sketched in this shorthand way? If so, should we focus our attention on F. Scott

QUESTION
How does the presence of this list of names affect the way you read the novel at this point?

CONTEXT
It is significant that Gatsby managed to achieve social advancement through war service. In 1840, in the second volume of his study *Democracy in America*, Alexis de Tocqueville (1805–59) remarked that in aristocratic societies military rank reflected social rank; however, in democratic armies, all soldiers might rise to officer class, and so assert their superiority over others through means closed to them during peacetime. He concluded that while democratic nations strove for peace, they secretly wished to wage war.

Fitzgerald at work, the author who gave plant names too to Daisy, Myrtle and Carraway, or on Nick the narrator, acutely aware of stylistic issues in his storytelling and here indulging in a little mischievous wordplay?

The rest of this chapter is emphatically concerned with the reconstruction of past events, and with how the **point of view** of the teller modifies the character of the account, and even its essential details. For example, Gatsby's comment that Jordan Baker is 'a great sportswoman' who would 'never do anything that wasn't all right' (p. 70) contradicts directly the conclusion arrived at by Nick in the previous chapter, and dramatically illustrates how interpretations may differ radically according to point of view. Gatsby's judgement is coloured by the fact that he is using Jordan to arrange a meeting with Daisy, and so he wants Nick to trust her.

More dramatically, Nick's perception of Meyer Wolfshiem is markedly different from the view held by Gatsby. In the narrative, Wolfshiem's reconstruction of the death of Rosy Rosenthal follows Gatsby's account of his own history and precedes Jordan's recollection of her encounter with Daisy and the handsome young lieutenant. The placing in Nick's narrative of Wolfshiem's tale of violence amongst gangsters inevitably causes sinister overtones to reverberate into the framing glimpses of Gatsby's past. F. Scott Fitzgerald manages in this way to present Gatsby as the heroic soldier and as the innocent lover, while hinting at his corruption.

Our readiness as readers to recognise such indirect hints is in part due to Nick's explicitly stated doubts concerning Gatsby's own version of his story. He tells us that listening to this version 'was like skimming hastily through a dozen magazines' (p. 65). The **simile** is highly appropriate to this phase of American history, when illustrated magazines promoted society gossip and helped create Hollywood legends, while also serving the requirements of modern advertising. Nick is suggesting that although an image of Gatsby's past has become visible, the reality behind it is far from distinct.

The Founding Fathers of modern America, who signed the Declaration of Independence in 1776, were adamant that it would be a peaceful nation; American history, however, is replete with conflict. Ironically, the success of Major Gatsby, promoted while active in a European war, is further evidence of the failure of fundamental American ideals with which F. Scott Fitzgerald is concerned in this novel (see **American ideals** in **Themes**).

On the journey into the city, Nick notices Americans originating from south-eastern Europe attending a funeral, and black Americans in an expensive car, driven by a white chauffeur. Both images obliquely foreshadow Gatsby's fate, while highlighting the fact that America is composed of people from various racial and cultural backgrounds. The materially successful black Americans may seem to suggest the existence of equal opportunities for social advancement. It is more likely in this context, where social injustice and obstacles to advancement are primary concerns, that F. Scott Fitzgerald is inviting us to suspect illegal means, as in the case of the Jewish gangster, Meyer Wolfshiem, and as in the case of the poor Midwestern farmer's son, James Gatz (see **Historical background**).

The murder of Herman 'Rosy' Rosenthal was an actual event, and it is one of the great strengths of the book that F. Scott Fitzgerald manages to fuse real historical occurrences with the stuff of romance. He is registering some of the social realities of America in the 1920s and at the same time is revealing impalpable beliefs, prejudices and desires that shaped events and granted different shades of meaning to contemporary interpretations of the physical facts.

Technically, the chapter makes bold use of abrupt transitions, notably the switch from Gatsby's meeting with Tom to Nick's conversation with Jordan, which is made with a cut that might have been modelled on cinematic practice.

Jordan recalls her meeting with Daisy, five years previously. Daisy's surname prior to her marriage was Fay. His biographers tell us that an important early influence upon F. Scott Fitzgerald's view of life was a priest named Father Cyril Sigourney Webster Fay. This may be the source of this character's name, but it is surely significant that 'fay' is an old English word for fairy, which is appropriate to an inhabitant of an enchanted world, as Daisy, in Gatsby's eyes, appears to be. Of course, Daisy's own romance world of nightingales and roses is actually artificial, and barely conceals an

> **CONTEXT**
> Wolfshiem was based closely upon an actual criminal called Arnold Rothstein, a professional gambler who was said to have fixed the outcome of the 1919 baseball World Series by bribing players to lose. Another literary character, Nathan Detroit, in the short-story collection *Guys and Dolls* (1932) by Damon Runyon (1884–1946), was also modelled on Rothstein.

CONTEXT

The 1920s was an important decade in cinema history. In 1927 Alan Crosland (1894–1936) directed *The Jazz Singer*, the first 'talkie'. Films were still silent when *The Great Gatsby* was written but there were skilled and serious directors at work making great advances in technique, and novelists, including F. Scott Fitzgerald, were quick to learn from their innovations. The year in which the novel is set, 1922, saw the release of *Orphans of the Storm*, an epic set during the French Revolution, directed by D. W. Griffith (1875–1948).

CONTEXT

What does the episode with Pammy tell us about Daisy's character?

unpalatable reality. We are lead to suspect that beneath its surface delicacy Daisy's character is tough and unfeeling.

When Nick grasps the nature of Gatsby's love for Daisy he remarks, 'He came alive to me, delivered suddenly from the womb of his purposeless splendour' (p. 76). He means that Gatsby became for him another person than the flashy character he had taken him for, showy with no purpose other than showiness. A passionate man has emerged unexpectedly from that inconsequential 'womb of purposeless splendour'

There are several comparable images of birth or rebirth in the novel, serving the theme of creating the self anew. Invariably they are as **ironic** as the suggestion of fertility in the word 'Egg' when applied to sterile rock. James Gatz has abandoned his actual mother, and when we see Daisy with her daughter, the novel's only instance of a maternal relationship, she displays a startling lack of motherly attachment.

It should be noted that in 1917 Daisy was just eighteen, and Jordan only sixteen. So, at the time the novel is set they are both still young. Jordan is just twenty-one, yet she is characterised by cynicism and scepticism. Despite this, Nick's amorous involvement with her develops during this chapter. We are invited to recognise that there is more emotional depth and sensuality to Nick than is suggested by his self-characterisation. He persistently presents himself as detached and rather cold but here he physically holds and kisses Jordan Baker. It may be that her world-weariness makes it difficult for him to cast a romantic light on their affair. Certainly, it is thematically useful for F. Scott Fitzgerald to contrast the reality of an attachment to someone who is materially there for Nick with Gatsby's elevated passion for an idealised and distant object of desire.

GLOSSARY

60	**bootlegger** someone involved in the illegal production and distribution of alcoholic drink. Prohibition of alcohol was current in America (see **Historical background**)
	Von Hindenburg Paul von Hindenburg (1847–1934), soldier and second president of Germany

GLOSSARY

64	**the Argonne Forest** in 1918 American troops were engaged in combat in this region of north-east France, close to the Belgian border
65	**little Montenegro** a small, mountainous kingdom, which in 1918 became part of Yugoslavia
	'Orderi di Danilo' … 'Nicolas Rex' King Danilo I ruled Montenegro from 1696 until 1735; Nicolas I was king from 1878 until 1918
66	**jug-jug-*spat*!** in his poem 'The Nightingale' (1798), Samuel Taylor Coleridge (1772–1834), following poetic convention, describes the bird's song as 'musical and swift jug jug'. F. Scott Fitzgerald is here deflating that Romantic convention, and in doing so passes tacit judgement upon Daisy, who earlier has claimed, unrealistically, to hear a nightingale in her garden
67	**the Queensboro Bridge** this bridge spans the East River, joining Queens and Manhattan
	Blackwell's Island an island that lies beneath the Queensboro Bridge, in the East River
68	**The old Metropole** a hotel at Broadway and Forty Third Street in Manhattan
	Rosy Rosenthal Herman Rosenthal testified against police corruption in New York. He was murdered in June 1912 by a gang which included a police officer, Charlie Becker. The killers, including Becker, were executed in 1915
71	**He's the man who fixed the World's Series back in 1919** in 1919 the Chicago White Sox baseball team accepted a bribe from an underworld gang to lose a game, and so allow the Cincinnati Reds to win the World Series championship
73	**Camp Taylor** in 1918 F. Scott Fitzgerald was stationed at Camp Zachary Taylor, near Louisville, Kentucky
75	**Santa Barbara** a fashionable resort on the coast of California, north of Los Angeles
76	**I'm the Sheik of Araby** 'The Sheik of Araby', written by Ted Snyder, with lyrics by Harry Smith and Francis Wheeler, was a popular song during 1921

www. CHECK THE NET
To see how the 'Orderi di Danilo' actually looked, visit http://public.srce.hr/hpm/p0170003.htm

www. CHECK THE NET
A brief summary of this lamentable event in baseball history can be found at http://1919blacksox.com/worldseries.htm

CHAPTER 5

- Nick organises a meeting at his house between Gatsby and Daisy.
- Gatsby then gives them a guided tour of his house, displaying his possessions, especially his expensive, imported clothes.

Late at night, Gatsby's house is brightly lit. He and Nick discuss the planned meeting with Daisy. On the agreed day, it is raining heavily. Leaving Gatsby and Daisy to renew acquaintance, Nick wanders into his garden and for half an hour contemplates Gatsby's mansion. He recalls that the house was built by a brewer, who aspired to be a kind of feudal lord, with his workers housed in thatched cottages. He returns to the room to find that Daisy has been crying.

Alone with Nick, Gatsby discloses that the money which bought his mansion was made in just three years. Then, with Daisy, they go to look at the house. The interior contains a range of items imported from Europe. Gatsby has clothes sent from England. Daisy is overwhelmed by his 'beautiful shirts' (p. 89).

Nick muses on the nature of Gatsby's desire for this woman, and remarks on the intensity of their relationship. Eventually, he leaves them alone together.

COMMENTARY

It should not escape our attention that as the encounter between the former lovers takes place, Nick says that he is 'Aware of the loud beating of my own heart' (p. 83). He evidently shares Gatsby's nervousness. We might ask why this should be so. It seems to illuminate the kind of identification Nick is making with Gatsby. Portraying himself as rather dull, starting to lose his hair, his head full of matters derived from the world of finance, Nick seems to take vicarious pleasure in Gatsby's doomed life as romantic hero.

Nick is transforming the man into a larger than life mythic figure when he describes Gatsby as being 'like an ecstatic patron of recurrent light' (p. 86). But in spite of the heightened style of his account there are moments that reveal a close personal identification, when he seems to share in Gatsby's pleasure and pain.

American nostalgia for the hierarchic society of Europe is evident in Gatsby's mansion, and its history. It has a 'feudal silhouette' (p. 88), outlined ironically by up-to-date electric lighting. The brewer who had it built aspired to be a feudal lord. Feudal society seems unjust to modern democratic sensibilities, yet it is evident that in early twentieth-century America, wealthy individuals were keen to assert their superiority, to proclaim their status in ways at odds with the egalitarian ideal. The characteristic quality of feudal life was stability. Relationships between the ruling class of lords and the peasantry remained unchanged through generations. It is ironic then that a citizen in a modern capitalist state, whose characteristic quality is change, dynamism, the creation of new markets and new modes of production, should desire to imitate the feudal set-up.

Nick observes, 'Americans, while willing, even eager, to be serfs, have always been obstinate about being peasantry' (p. 86). The distinction between a serf and a peasant is a fine one, as both terms imply a condition of servitude, enforced labour and obedience to a master. Nick may be suggesting that while Americans might in effect be drudges at work, they would resist being openly cast in a peasant role, which immediately suggests the stark inequalities of medieval European society.

Nick works professionally as a bondsman, managing financial bonds. An older meaning of bondsman was a labourer bound to a master, in other words a 'serf'. Through this simple wordplay F. Scott Fitzgerald casts further ironic light upon America's purported clean break from the European past.

Discussing the impact that Daisy has made upon Gatsby during their reunion, Nick comments, 'After his embarrassment and his unreasoning joy he was consumed with wonder at her presence' (p. 89). 'Wonder' is a key word in the novel, and it recurs with amplified significance at the end, where it is inspired by a dramatic first encounter with the American continent.

CHECK THE BOOK

Tony Tanner's *The Reign of Wonder* (CUP, 1965) offers a broad consideration of 'wonder', blending innocence and vision, as an important and recurrent quality in American literature.

CONTEXT

Dan Cody shares his surname with William F. Cody (1846–1917), popularly known as 'Buffalo Bill', a showman who turned the 'Wild West' into a public spectacle with carefully staged shows involving cowboys and 'Indians', as Native Americans were called, enacting stereotypical roles. F. Scott Fitzgerald was clearly making use of that association with a recently deceased historical figure.

CHAPTER 6

- Nick reveals more about Gatsby's past, his humble origins and his time with Dan Cody.
- The Buchanans attend one of Gatsby's parties, and the growing tension between Tom and his host is evident.

Nick introduces more details to form a picture of Gatsby's past. His original name was James Gatz, changed when he was seventeen to the more glamorous Jay Gatsby. He came from North Dakota, a state on the border with Canada and situated midway between the East and West Coasts of America.

His real break with the past came when Dan Cody moored his yacht in the shallows of Lake Superior, and Gatz warned him of possible danger from high wind. It was at this point that the new name came into being, to match the beauty and glamour which Cody's yacht represented to him. Gatsby was rewarded with an education in the ways of the world from this opportunist millionaire, 'a product of the Nevada silver fields, of the Yukon, of every rush for metal since seventy-five' (p. 96).

Nick discusses the act of self-creation that produced the man he calls 'The Great Gatsby'. This idealistic act is in stark contrast to the relentless materialism of Cody, who yet became Gatsby's 'destiny' (p. 96). During his five years as Cody's assistant, Gatsby sailed three times around the American continent. Then Cody died. Gatsby's legacy was not the twenty-five thousands dollars Cody intended he should inherit but a 'singularly appropriate education' (p. 97). Nick holds this, rather than contesting rumours, to be the authentic history.

He then reports an occasion when Tom was brought as a guest to Gatsby's mansion. Gatsby told Tom that he knew his wife. Tom's response was to make the edgy remark: 'I may be old-fashioned in my ideas, but women run around too much these days to suit me' (p. 100).

The narrative shifts to the following Saturday, when the Buchanans attend Gatsby's party. Tom suggests to Nick that Gatsby is a bootlegger. Gatsby wants Daisy to leave her husband for him and to tell Tom that she never loved him. Nick warns, 'You can't repeat the past'; but Gatsby replies, 'Why of course you can!' (p. 106), illustrating a capacity to delude himself commensurate with his boundless capacity for hope.

CONTEXT

During the last quarter of the nineteenth century discoveries of readily accessible mineral ores caused prospectors to rush to make their fortunes. The Yukon Territory, in the far north, saw a rush for gold, and Nevada, in the west, saw a rush for silver. In both cases the dream of getting rich quickly was the motivation. The reality was often disappointment and hardship.

CONTEXT
The 1920s was the decade of 'the flapper', the young woman who exercised unprecedented freedom, having short hair, wearing a relatively short skirt and applying make-up of a kind that previously had suggested immorality. Greatly increased mobility, in search of pleasure, was characteristic of the flapper, and it was F. Scott Fitzgerald in short stories such as those in the collection *Flappers and Philosophers* (1920) who introduced this new kind of female into literature.

CHECK THE BOOK
R. W. B. Lewis's *The American Adam: Innocence, Tragedy, and Tradition in the Nineteenth Century* (University of Chicago Press, 1955) and Leo Marx's *The Machine in the Garden: Technology and the Pastoral Ideal in America* (OUP, 1964) are classic studies that offer different perspectives on the tradition of conceiving the New World as an Eden.

Jay Gatsby's ideal future is in fact the restoration of a golden moment from his past, rather than something truly new and unprecedented. Compare the claims made by early American settlers that their New World offered the opportunity to return to the Garden of Eden. Utopian thinking, the concept of an ideal future, has often proved to be little more than a form of nostalgia for a Golden Age, supposed to have existed in the distant past. This tradition itself goes back a long way. The ancient Greek poet Hesiod (eighth century BC), for example, in his poem *Works and Days* traced a decline from a Golden Age, when people lived without sorrow, through a Silver Age, Bronze Age and Heroic Age to the corrupted and troubled present, which he termed the Iron Age.

COMMENTARY

F. Scott Fitzgerald here picks up the concern with capacity for wonder introduced in the previous chapter. Here he makes explicit the childlike quality of innocent vision which must accompany it. In Gatsby's eyes the city streets become trees, transformed into a green world by means of imagination and intense feeling. Gatsby feels he can climb those trees, and at their top he can 'suck on the pap of life, gulp down the incomparable milk of wonder' (p. 107).

The nurturing breast that is figured here as 'the pap of life' is echoed at the end of the book in the image of the 'fresh, green breast of the new world' (Chapter 9, p. 171). In between these moments of vision, one of Myrtle Wilson's breasts is mutilated in an automobile accident. F. Scott Fitzgerald contrasts the capacity of **metaphor** to create a visionary reality with a brutal, physical reality that constantly threatens to undermine the power of the vision. The possibility of sustaining a vision that might redeem the world from cruelty and suffering is a major concern in the narrative.

Gatsby has transformed himself from a humble Midwestern boy to an East Coast celebrity. He has also transformed Daisy Fay, within his own imagination, from a Southern girl to an ideal of radiant life and beauty. The novel is packed with references to magic and to enchantment, and, at least within the confines of his own mind, 'The Great Gatsby' is an accomplished magician. The phrase

'The Great Gatsby' carries a suggestion of the showmanship of stage magicians, who practise an art of illusion and use such names to advertise their performances.

Dan Cody, Gatsby's mentor, transformed himself into a millionaire, but underneath the veneer of material success he remained 'the pioneer debauchee, who during one phase of American life brought back to the Eastern seaboard the savage violence of the frontier brothel and saloon' (p. 97). F. Scott Fitzgerald is here deflating an idealised version of pioneer life, characterised by heroism and high-mindedness. Just as Gatsby casts his world in a romantic light, so America has imagined its Western past in elevated terms. That illusion is dispelled with this honest look at Cody. The satirist Mark Twain (1835–1910) had earlier produced a much fuller deflation of the prospecting life of the American West in *Roughing It* (1872), a work which F. Scott Fitzgerald knew well. There is ambivalence in F. Scott Fitzgerald's attitude towards imagination: it can be seen to work magic and make ordinary life seem enchanted; or it can be seen to generate illusions that keep harsh realities out of focus and help perpetuate injustices.

In contrast to Cody's materialism, we are told that Gatsby created himself according to a Platonic conception. Plato's philosophy stresses the illusory nature of the world that we know through our physical senses, and insists upon the ultimate reality of an ideal world. Anti-democratic and opposed to materialism, such a Platonic conception seems to be fundamentally out of step with modern American priorities. F. Scott Fitzgerald recognised, however, that despite rampant materialist values, twentieth-century Americans often clung to an ideal sense of their own national and personal destinies. This ideal sense is embodied in Jay Gatsby, caught up in property and money yet driven by desire for something beyond physical possessions.

We may see Nick's role as writer as the process of extending Gatsby's transforming vision so that we may all share in it. In other words, Nick as writer is able to emulate his hero's power to change base materials into something of lasting value, in a way that Nick the bondsman, and even Nick the lover, is not. Gatsby meets

CONTEXT

The best-known magician amongst F. Scott Fitzgerald's contemporaries was Harry Houdini (1874–1926), who changed his name from Erich Weiss. That change may be compared perhaps with James Gatz's adoption of the name Jay Gatsby. Houdini achieved fame as an escapologist and featured in silent films including *The Master Mystery* and *The Grim Game*.

CONTEXT

In *The Republic*, his blueprint for a model society, the ancient Greek philosopher Plato (c.427–347BC) argues that the material world is illusory and that true reality is an ideal realm, which our physical organs of sense are too crude to apprehend. He compares the common experience of everyday things to being trapped in a cave watching shadows cast on a wall by a light source that cannot be seen directly. Only a philosophical elite, he claims, has intuitive access to this ideal reality.

CHECK THE BOOK

F. Scott Fitzgerald's English contemporary D. H. Lawrence (1885–1930) wrote an insightful book, *Studies in Classic American Literature* (1923), in which he identifies 'plumbing' and 'saving the World' as 'the two great American specialities'. He connects these practical and visionary aspects of American culture, arguing that the national aptitude for inventing labour-saving machines is actually a means to the end of freeing time for dreaming.

his physical death at the hands of George Wilson, who is crazed by the killing of his wife, but Gatsby lives on in the realm of literature, in the book that Nick is writing and, of course, in F. Scott Fitzgerald's novel.

GLOSSARY

94   **'underground pipe-line to Canada'** it was rumoured during Prohibition that a pipeline existed to channel alcohol from Canada into the United States

95   *Tuolomee* named after a gold-mining area in the Sierra Nevada mountains of northern California

     Platonic conception Plato (c.427–347BC) was a Greek philosopher, who argued that the material world was illusory, and that true reality existed in an ideal realm beyond the reach of the human senses

     he must be about His Father's Business an ironic allusion to the words of Jesus, reported in the gospel of St Luke 2:49

96   **Madame de Maintenon** (1635–1719) she was the second wife of Louis XIV, and influenced major decisions of state

CHAPTER 7

- Nick and Gatsby visit the Buchanans', where Jordan is also a guest, and meet Daisy's daughter.
- En route to the city, the group stops at George Wilson's garage, and Wilson discloses that he and his wife are planning to go West.
- The group takes a room at the Plaza Hotel, where Tom and Gatsby argue about which of them Daisy loves.
- Myrtle Wilson is killed by a hit-and-run driver.
- Gatsby reveals to Nick that Daisy was driving the vehicle, but announces his intention to take the blame.

There have been changes of staff at Gatsby's house, apparently to ensure discretion concerning Daisy's visits. On the hottest day of the summer, Nick takes up an invitation to visit the Buchanans', where Jordan is also a guest. A nurse brings Daisy's daughter, Pammy, to meet Nick and Gatsby. Daisy suggests that the adults should go to town. She discloses her love for Gatsby through her manner, her 'indiscreet voice', but also tells him he resembles in his coolness a certain advertisement. Gatsby notes that her voice is 'full of money' (p. 115).

Tom drives Nick and Jordan to town in Gatsby's car and discloses that he has been investigating Gatsby's past. He denies that Gatsby actually attended Oxford University. Jordan accuses Tom of snobbery.

They stop for petrol at George Wilson's garage. Wilson says that he is unwell and that he and Myrtle are planning to go West. Tom is startled by this news. Wilson has recognised that his wife has been having an affair, although he seems to be unaware that Tom is involved. Nick notices Myrtle looking from a window. He reads in her face jealousy at the sight of Jordan, whom she takes to be Tom's wife. Tom feels both his wife and his mistress are slipping away from him.

Tom, Nick, Daisy, Jordan and Gatsby take a room in the glamorous and exclusive Plaza Hotel. Amid tense banter the sound of the Wedding March is heard, recalling to Daisy her marriage in Louisville, Kentucky, in June, some years before. Gatsby, challenged by Tom, explains that he spent five months in Oxford in 1919, as part of a special arrangement made for members of the American armed forces in Europe. Tom, deploring Gatsby's advances to Daisy, calls him 'Mr Nobody from Nowhere' (p. 123). Things come to a head with Gatsby declaring that Daisy loves him rather than her husband, and claiming that it was because he was poor that they did not marry.

After denying her love for Tom, Daisy eventually admits that she has loved him in the past. It becomes clear that the past five years, since Tom intervened between the youthful lovers, cannot simply be erased. Gatsby still insists that Daisy is leaving Tom for him.

? QUESTION
What are the implications of Gatsby's observation that Daisy's voice is 'full of money'?

CONTEXT
Horace Greeley (1811–72), editor of the *New York Tribune*, famously offered the advice 'Go West!' to Americans seeking opportunities for self-advancement. The phrase became a popular slogan, but westward movement had long been associated with American hope for a new beginning and boundless potential.

CONTEXT

Louisville is the largest city in the state of Kentucky. It was founded in 1778 and named after King Louis XVI of France, a monarch beheaded in 1793 following the French Revolution. It is best known as the location since 1875 of the Kentucky Derby, the most popular spectacle in American horse racing. A pleasing incidental detail is that a horse named Buchanan won the event in 1884.

Then Tom suggests that Gatsby has made money from bootlegging, in association with Wolfshiem. Following this it is clear that Gatsby has lost Daisy irretrievably; this is a critical turning point in his life.

Nick remembers that it is his thirtieth birthday, and considers his own prospects to be bleak.

The narrative shifts to a character named Michaelis, who is introduced as 'the principal witness at the inquest' (p. 129). F. Scott Fitzgerald may have derived that name, Michaelis, from Joseph Conrad's novel *The Secret Agent* (1907), where it belongs to a grotesquely fat anarchist. The novel's pivotal event has occurred. Wilson and Myrtle had an argument. In her anger, distracted, Myrtle rushed into the street and was fatally injured by a car. The car did not stop. Nick gives an account of his own arrival at the scene, with Tom driving. A bystander testifies that the 'death car' (p. 131) was a big yellow vehicle.

The narrative cuts to the Buchanans' home, where Nick meets Gatsby in the garden. Gatsby reveals that Daisy was driving the car that killed Myrtle, but says that he intends to take the blame. It seems that Myrtle mistakenly thought Tom was at the wheel of the yellow car. Nick returns to the house and finds Tom and Daisy sharing 'an unmistakable air of natural intimacy' (p. 138). They appear to be hatching a conspiracy. Nick leaves Gatsby at his customary vigil, fixated on the green electric light at the end of Daisy's dock, 'watching over nothing' (p. 139).

COMMENTARY

After the image of the nurturing maternal breast noted in the last chapter, Daisy's inadequacies as a mother are especially striking. Her daughter, Pammy, is displayed like one more possession in a household wealthy enough to employ a nurse, along with numerous other servants.

The class distinction between the wealthy and their employees is subsequently invoked by Tom in order to assert his superiority over Gatsby, and to emphasise Gatsby's unsuitability as a suitor to Daisy.

He says, 'I'll be damned if I see how you got within a mile of her unless you brought the groceries to the back door' (p. 125).

The party at the Plaza Hotel forms a structural echo of the drinking session at Myrtle's apartment in Chapter 2. These small parties are interspersed with the larger affairs organised by Gatsby, and effectively provide a close-up sequence, or narrowing of focus from the more panoramic events on West Egg. In these set pieces, F. Scott Fitzgerald demonstrates his skill in creating dramatic exchanges in dialogue, using speech to advance the action and to deepen our understanding of the characters and their motivation (see **Dialogue and the scenic method** in **Techniques**).

In one such exchange, Tom accuses Gatsby of being 'Mr Nobody from Nowhere' (p. 123). Given the rootless drifting that seems to characterise the lifestyle of the Buchanans and their class, this criticism might seem misguided. But Tom is really asserting that America belongs to him and to his kind, and that this upstart who has bypassed the orthodox channels to social respectability has no claim to recognition. **Utopia**, the term for an ideal society, is derived from ancient Greek words meaning 'nowhere'. Gatsby is, in a sense, a utopian figure, materially successful yet, as Nick portrays him, also an ideal figure, not simply defined by his possessions but transcending them in his singular capacity for hope.

Tom's pretensions to an older, aristocratic order are evident in his boast of being 'the first man who ever made a stable out of a garage' (p. 113). He takes advantage of the many conveniences that come with modernity, cars and telephones assist his adultery, but he is hostile to the essentially democratic implications of technological modernisation. The stable contains the polo ponies that are indicative of his status as a member of a leisure class, so wealthy that he does not need to work. George Wilson, on the other hand, depends on his garage for survival.

F. Scott Fitzgerald took care over his choice of names for characters. Daisy and Myrtle have plant names corresponding to their personal characteristics, the delicate flower and the hardy shrub. Jordan Baker's name combines two makes of automobile, reinforcing her role in the book as an unequivocally modern woman. George

CHECK THE BOOK

A fascinating account of pre-twentieth-century communitarian experiments is Mark Holloway's *Heavens on Earth: Utopian Communities in America, 1680–1880* (Dover Publications, 1966). Holloway conveys the sense of boundless hope that drove these experiments and which lingers in F. Scott Fitzgerald's character Jay Gatsby.

Wilson's name may similarly bear resonant associations. Woodrow Wilson (1856–1924) was president of the United States between 1913 and 1921 and took America into the First World War. George Washington (1732–99) was America's first president between 1789 and 1797. George Wilson's name may evoke these two eminent figures but the garage owner resides nonetheless in the dismal 'valley of ashes' (Chapter 2, p. 26).

Nick's recollection that it is his thirtieth birthday provides an insight into the melancholy side of his character: 'Thirty – the promise of a decade of loneliness, a thinning list of single men to know, a thinning brief-case of enthusiasm, thinning hair' (p. 129). F. Scott Fitzgerald suggested, with a degree of seriousness, that life goes downhill after you have reached the age of fifteen. He was keenly aware that the intensity of youthful expectations and aspirations, the largely undefined sense of hope one has in childhood, can be eroded steadily by accumulated experience and steady disappointment. Jay Gatsby, we are told, is the adolescent creation of James Gatz, and that youthful outlook, not jaded by the responsibilities and obligations of adulthood despite the intervening years and experience of war, remains Gatsby's distinguishing characteristic.

CHECK THE BOOK

Matthew J. Bruccoli's biography *Some Sort of Epic Grandeur: The Life of F. Scott Fitzgerald* (Harcourt Brace Jovanovich, 1981; paperback, Cardinal Books, 1991) sheds light on this aspect of F. Scott Fitzgerald's temperament.

Nick's dismal vision of diminishing potential contrasts markedly with his earlier statement of appreciation for Gatsby's 'heightened sensitivity to the promises of life' (Chapter 1, p. 8). His sense of his own mortality, an irreversible movement towards his own death, is captured in an **ambivalent** sentence that also foreshadows the discovery of Myrtle Wilson's body: 'So we drove on toward death through the cooling twilight' (p. 129).

The grotesque description of Myrtle's mutilated body provides a horrifying contrast to earlier and later images of the nurturing breast: 'her left breast was swinging loose like a flap, and there was no need to listen for the heart beneath' (p. 131). This statement also takes up the novel's concern with relationships between surface and depth, image and actuality. Here for once there is correspondence between the two; the mangled surface corresponds with the lifeless core.

The automobile, embodiment of freedom of movement and symbol of social as well as physical mobility, has become an instrument of death and mutilation as it does in other American novels of the time, such as Theodore Dreiser's *An American Tragedy* (1925) and Sinclair Lewis's *Elmer Gantry* (1927). The singularity of Gatsby's vehicle, its conspicuousness, makes tracing the culprit easy, and with a little assistance from Tom Buchanan, George Wilson soon finds his way to the Gatsby mansion.

CHECK THE FILM
A cinematic version of *An American Tragedy* was made in 1931, directed by Josef von Sternberg. *Elmer Gantry* was filmed in 1960, directed by Richard Brooks, with Burt Lancaster in the title role.

GLOSSARY	
108	**Trimalchio** a wealthy patron and extravagant host in the *Satyricon*, a satirical work by the Roman author Petronius (died 65AD). F. Scott Fitzgerald at one point considered calling his novel *Trimalchio in West Egg*
113	**blessed isles** in classical mythology, islands where eternal peace might be found
120	**mint julep** a drink made with bourbon, sugar and mint, served with ice, and very popular in the American South
120	**Kapiolani ... the Punch Bowl** parks in Honolulu, Hawaii, where the Buchanans spent their honeymoon

CHAPTER 8

- Nick has a sleepless night. He visits Gatsby, who tells him about his past, and the nature of his love for Daisy.
- George Wilson, desperate in his grief, kills Gatsby and then shoots himself.

Nick tells of his sleepless night, caught 'between grotesque reality and savage, frightening dreams' (p. 140). Towards dawn he visits Gatsby, advising him to leave home. Gatsby is determined to stay, to monitor Daisy's movements. Gatsby tells Nick of his youthful experiences with Cody – 'told it to me because "Jay Gatsby" had broken up like glass against Tom's hard malice, and the long secret extravaganza was played out' (p. 141). Nick shows Gatsby's fragile world to have been shattered by the insistent and brutally physical reality of Tom Buchanan.

Nick tells how Gatsby was overcome by desire on his youthful visits to Daisy Fay's home, which seemed to encapsulate the magical freshness of romance. His subsequent commitment to Daisy is described as 'the following of a grail' (p. 142).

Gatsby received the letter announcing Daisy's decision to marry Tom while he was at Oxford. In the days before transatlantic air travel became commonplace the distance from Oxford to Louisville, Kentucky, where the wedding took place, remained a large one and left Gatsby powerless to intervene.

Gatsby has asked his gardener to postpone the planned draining of his pool and has expressed his intention of swimming in it. Nick is reluctant to leave him. At noon, at work, Nick receives a call from Jordan Baker.

Nick shifts his narration to an account of George Wilson's despair, and his obsessive, distracted behaviour. Wilson tells Michaelis that Myrtle was murdered by her lover. He then mistakes the eyes of Doctor Eckleburg for those of an all-seeing God. He searches for the owner of the yellow car, is directed to Gatsby, and tracks him down.

Gatsby awaits a call from Daisy, but resignedly goes to the pool where he floats on a mattress. His death is presented obliquely – his chauffeur hears shots. His gardener finds Wilson dead in the grass. With his suicide, we are told, 'the holocaust was complete' (p. 154). The word 'holocaust' here indicates wholesale destruction.

COMMENTARY

In this chapter, Nick declares again that he disapproved of Gatsby 'from beginning to end' (pp. 146–7). Yet, in spite of this declared disapproval, the close identification with Gatsby implicit in his decision to write a book about him becomes more explicit. Nick's sympathy verges on the protectiveness of a parent towards an innocent child. This protectiveness may recall Nick's kindness to

> **CONTEXT**
>
> The Holy Grail was the cup from which Jesus Christ drank at the Last Supper and it was used by Joseph of Arimathea to catch Christ's blood as he hung from the Cross. The quest for the Grail became a major narrative element in the legends of King Arthur and his court. Sir Galahad was the knight who led the search for the sacred vessel. Jay Gatsby envisages his pursuit of Daisy in terms of chivalric romance that is quite at odds with the reality of twentieth-century America.

McKee, at the end of Chapter 2. There are numerous instances of this kind of structural echo in the novel (see **Intricate patterning** in **Techniques**).

Nick observes that in his disillusionment Gatsby 'must have felt that he had lost the old warm world, paid a high price for living too long with a single dream' (p. 153). There is a verbal echo here of Nick's earlier remark that after the war the Midwest was no longer for him 'the warm centre of the world' (Chapter 1, p. 9). There is a shared experience of displacement, which draws the men together. It might be seen as loss of home or, in biblical terms, as expulsion from Eden.

Nick makes an overt statement of the affinity he feels with Gatsby:

> 'They're a rotten crowd,' I shouted across the lawn. 'You're worth the whole damn bunch put together.'

> I've always been glad I said that. It was the only compliment I ever gave him, because I disapproved of him from beginning to end. First he nodded politely, and then his face broke into that radiant and understanding smile, as if we'd been in ecstatic cahoots on that fact all the time. (pp. 146–7)

The phrase 'in ecstatic cahoots' is extraordinary. It combines an American vernacular term, 'in cahoots', meaning 'in league with', and the adjective 'ecstatic' meaning to be 'in an exalted state' and derived from the ancient Greek words for 'standing outside of oneself'.

In Chapter 2, after drinking heavily, Nick describes himself as 'within and without, simultaneously enchanted and repelled by the inexhaustible variety of life' (Chapter 2, p. 37). Gatsby also has stood simultaneously 'within and without' and has known ecstatic states in a way that Nick at the same time mistrusts and greatly admires.

Such a divided response was not unknown to F. Scott Fitzgerald, who was both attracted to and yet deeply critical of the lifestyle of the very wealthy. His own **ambivalence** seems to inform the

CHECK THE BOOK

R. W. B. Lewis, in *The American Adam: Innocence, Tragedy, and Tradition in the Nineteenth Century* (University of Chicago Press, 1955), outlines a tradition in American writing of presenting the New World in terms of the Garden of Eden and the representative American as Adam. Gatsby, who attempts to erase the past and create himself anew, falls squarely, if ironically, into this tradition. Daisy might then be seen as Eve, the archetypal temptress.

declaration that 'Gatsby was overwhelmingly aware of the youth and mystery that wealth imprisons and preserves, of the freshness of many clothes, and of Daisy, gleaming like silver, safe and proud above the hot struggles of the poor' (p. 142). This sentence expresses desire for the advantages of wealth, while acknowledging that there is something inauthentic about this artificial preservation of 'freshness'. It also registers the discomforting existence of the poor.

Gatsby's own advancement, as we have seen, is entwined with historical events: 'He did extraordinarily well in the war' (p. 143). The war was the 'colossal accident' (p. 141) which took him to Camp Taylor and so led him to Daisy Fay. She became his grail, the sacred object of a quest undertaken, as in Arthurian **romance**, by a loyal and devoted knight. The young officer is thus transformed into a chivalric hero, a knight whose shining armour takes the form of immaculate suits and shirts, and whose steed is an expensive automobile.

George Wilson's identification of the eyes of Doctor Eckleburg with those of God is the most striking case of mistaken identity in the novel. F. Scott Fitzgerald seems to be suggesting that advertising is the real god of modern America, recreating the citizens of America in its own image (see **Historical background**).

As F. Scott Fitzgerald noted that novelist Joseph Conrad was his literary master during the writing of *The Great Gatsby*, it seems appropriate to point out that the indirect presentation of Gatsby's death (no melodramatic description, just a cry heard by a servant) is comparable to the death of Verloc in Joseph Conrad's *The Secret Agent* (1907). Verloc is stabbed by his wife. The incident is conveyed with great effectiveness through description of the shadow of her arm on a wall. Winnie Verloc subsequently commits suicide and, as is the case with George Wilson, the newspapers report the deaths as acts of madness.

CONTEXT

The Association of National Advertisers and the American Association of Advertising Agencies were established in 1910 and 1917 respectively.

CHECK THE BOOK

Susan Strasser's *Satisfaction Guaranteed: The Making of the American Mass Market* (Pantheon, 1989) includes a highly readable account of how advertising became during the early twentieth century a powerful means of influence and persuasion.

GLOSSARY

143	**'Beale Street Blues'** jazz tune written in 1917 by W. C. Handy (1873–1958), who was known as 'the Father of the Blues'
147	**Hempstead … Southampton** towns on Long Island

CHAPTER 9

- Gatsby's funeral takes place, with his father one of the very few mourners present.
- Henry Gatz speaks with pride of his son's attainments.
- Later, Nick contemplates the empty mansion and ponders the significance of Gatsby's story.

Nick is narrating in 1924, two years after the events of the story have occurred.

Following Gatsby's death Nick makes arrangements for the funeral, but despite the large number of guests who attended Gatsby's parties, people now stay away. It becomes clear that he was actually friendless. The Buchanans have left town, leaving no address. At Gatsby's mansion Nick receives a solitary telephone call, from one of Gatsby's underworld contacts, unaware that he is dead.

Eventually a telegram arrives from Henry C. Gatz. Then he arrives from a town in Minnesota, a colourless shabby figure, who has learnt of his son's death indirectly, from a Chicago newspaper.

The morning of the funeral, Nick visits Meyer Wolfshiem. He has received a brief note of commiseration from Wolfshiem but has been unable to reach him by telephone. Eventually, despite attempts by Wolfshiem's secretary to deter him, Nick gets to see the crooked gambler, who says he cannot attend the funeral.

QUESTION
How does the character of Henry Gatz, as we witness it here, modify your understanding of his son's character?

Back in West Egg, Gatz expresses pride in his son's attainments. Inside the house he shows Nick a photograph of it – the image 'was more real to him now than the house itself' (p. 163). It is the idea of the house, the mansion as a symbol of success and a reward for adherence to the principle of honest endeavour, that matters to the old man rather than its physical reality. He also shows Nick a copy of the book *Hopalong Cassidy* owned by Gatsby as a boy. It contains a schedule written by James Gatz to organise his days effectively.

No message is received from Daisy, and nobody attends the funeral except Nick, Gatsby's father, four or five servants, and the postman. The man Nick calls 'Owl Eyes' also turns up at the cemetery.

Nick's narration cuts to his recollections of returning West from prep school – his Midwest is not a place but a journey: 'the thrilling returning trains of my youth'. He realises that 'this has been a story of the West, after all' (p. 167).

He visits Jordan, who tells him she is engaged to another man. He doubts the veracity of this but feigns surprise. Jordan accuses him of being a bad driver after all: 'I thought you were rather an honest, straightforward person. I thought it was your secret pride' (p. 168). The word 'driver' links the world of automobiles with the world of golf, where a driver is a type of club. Jordan's phrase 'bad driver' evokes both the fatal car crash and her own history as an allegedly cheating golfer.

In late October, Nick encounters Tom Buchanan on Fifth Avenue. Tom admits to telling George Wilson that Gatsby owned the car that killed Myrtle.

Before leaving for the Midwest, Nick recalls Gatsby's parties and contemplates the house, recognising that in every sense 'the party was over' (p. 171). He erases with his shoe an obscene word inscribed by a boy with a piece of brick. Nick, soon to transform himself into a writer, is sensitive to the power of language to violate the past; he wants his own carefully chosen words to attach to Gatsby's memory, not some uncouth scrawl. Then he goes to the beach, and in the moonlight he has a vision of Dutch sailors encountering this new world for the first time. He refers to Gatsby's faith in 'the orgastic future' (p. 171) and considers more generally the fate of human hopes and aspirations.

COMMENTARY

Two years have elapsed between Nick's departure from West Egg and this moment of writing the concluding chapter of his account. We know nothing of Nick's life in the meantime, but it seems that he has dedicated much of his time to reliving the experience of those New York years through the process of literary composition. In the course of this, he has preserved the figure of Jay Gatsby for posterity.

Inevitably, in the act of writing, Nick has entered into isolation. This may be a further reflection of his identification with Gatsby, who was isolated not only after his death (when nearly everyone abandoned him), but even at those parties, where he stood apart, simultaneously the host and a detached onlooker. If isolation was the price of Gatsby's idealism, it seems that Nick Carraway is prepared to accept similar isolation as the price for literary creativity, a process through which he hopes to open a window onto a world of ideals.

Nick recognises that he has written a story of the West, by which he means a story that addresses the fate of American ideals. He stresses that for him the West was the journey westward rather than arrival home. In the terms of American mythology, the West has signified a condition of continual becoming, rather than a stale state of being. The **mythical** America envisaged by early settlers was a utopian place where life could be constantly begun anew, a place of limitless possibility for personal fulfilment and self-realisation (see **American ideals** in **Themes**). Gatsby, despite the flaws and contradictions in his character, preserves this ideal, and it is summed up in his belief in 'the green light, the orgastic future' (p. 171).

The green electric light at the end of Daisy's dock may seem trivial when compared to the fresh green breast of America encountered by early settlers, and in a sense it is, but, charged with the intensity of Gatsby's vision, that light preserves symbolically the same values of hope, dream and desire that the New World held for those settlers. The green light sustained its enchantment as long as Gatsby did not actually manage to grasp it. As long as it remained something to long for, at a distance, it retained its magical potency. In a touching parallel to this, Henry Gatz shows Nick a photograph of his son's mansion, while they are actually in the mansion. The image, and the ideal of fulfilment it stands for, had enchanted Gatz from a distance; the real thing is unable to exercise the same power: 'the green light, the orgastic future' is infinitely more than the small glowing object across the water that Gatsby brooded over night after night.

Jordan's accusation that Nick is a 'bad driver', with its other association of a poor golfer failing to drive the ball towards the hole that is his target, has a grim resonance following Myrtle's death

www. CHECK THE NET
An indication of the role played by the Dutch in the early settlement of America's East Coast can be found at **http://www.state. dc.us/sos/dpa/ exhibits/document/ 17th/bakdutch.shtml**

in an automobile accident. Nick has taken pride in his own honesty and carefulness, while branding Jordan reckless and fundamentally dishonest. Does this sudden reversal tell us that he really is not the kind of man he has seemed to be all along? Does it reveal that he has much more in common with the passionate Gatsby than his characteristic reticence would suggest? If so, then maybe we should return to the beginning and reread his account, in order to see things more clearly. *The Great Gatsby* is certainly a book that invites rereading, and invariably repays it with new disclosures.

The novel ends with a passage which has become a universally acknowledged classic of American writing (see **Text 5** in **Extended commentaries**).

CHECK THE NET

The F. Scott Fitzgerald centenary web site – **http://www.sc.edu/ fitzgerald** – has many interesting sections, including fascinating facts and anecdotes about the author and his work.

GLOSSARY	
155	**adventitious** not direct. As in so many cases in the novel, a judgement has been relayed through the voices of others, rather than directly experienced
	pasquinade lampoon or **satire**. It is notable that F. Scott Fitzgerald gives such vocabulary to Nick, indicating the sophistication of a Yale graduate, and a real concern for language, despite the fact that he describes himself as a rather dull dealer in bonds
160	**James J. Hill** (1838–1916) an extremely wealthy business ally of John Pierpont Morgan, who rose from humble origins. He ran the Great Northern Railway, which was based in St Paul (where F. Scott Fitzgerald was born), and in the spirit of earlier pioneers drove it across the wilderness to the West Coast of the continent. F. Scott Fitzgerald felt particular admiration for him
	Greenwich a wealthy suburb of New York City
161	**The Swastika Holding Company** the swastika was adopted by the Nazi party, but previously it had been a symbol of good fortune in India
	'The Rosary' a song written in 1898, which became popular in the 1920s
162	**the American Legion** an organisation for veterans of the US armed forces, formed in 1919

GLOSSARY

164	*Hopalong Cassidy* a cowboy book by Clarence E. Mulford published in 1910
	SCHEDULE F. Scott Fitzgerald based James Gatz's schedule on that in Benjamin Franklin's *Autobiography* (1818), which exemplified the American faith in advancement through self-discipline and hard work
167	**El Greco** (1541–1614) a Spanish painter of religious scenes, whose figures tended to appear elongated and so curiously distorted
171	**orgastic** another example of Nick's extensive vocabulary, this is an alternative version of orgasmic. When Maxwell Perkins queried this word, F. Scott Fitzgerald explained that it was the adjective from 'orgasm', and it was intended to express a state of ecstasy. Orgasm, as a culminating moment of sexual excitement, suggests intense experience which seems to stand outside the flow of historical time. Some editions of the novel mistakenly preserve 'orgiastic' (the adjective from 'orgy'), which was an unauthorised and incorrect change made by Edmund Wilson in 1941, after F. Scott Fitzgerald's death

CONTEXT

Hopalong Cassidy (1910) was a Western tale written by Clarence E. Mulford (1883–1956). It proved so popular that numerous further books featuring the cowboy hero followed, films were made, starting in 1934, and later there was a television series. The schedule found inside the book is modelled on a famous plan for efficient organisation of each day in Benjamin Franklin's posthumously published *Autobiography* (1818). Franklin (1706–90) was one of America's Founding Fathers and a prominent advocate of hard work, honesty and discipline as the keys to spiritual and material success.

EXTENDED COMMENTARIES

TEXT 1 – PP. 17–18 (CHAPTER 1)

'We ought to plan something,' yawned Miss Baker, sitting down at the table as if she were getting into bed.

'All right,' said Daisy. 'What'll we plan?' She turned to me helplessly: 'What do people plan?'

Before I could answer her eyes fastened with an awed expression on her little finger.

'Look!' she complained; 'I hurt it.'

We all looked – the knuckle was black and blue.

 CHECK THE NET

For more information about Hopalong Cassidy visit **http://www. hopalong.com/ legend.htm**

'You did it, Tom,' she said accusingly. 'I know you didn't mean to, but you *did* do it. That's what I get for marrying a brute of a man, a great, big, hulking physical specimen of a –'

'I hate that word hulking,' objected Tom crossly, 'even in kidding.'

'Hulking,' insisted Daisy.

Sometimes she and Miss Baker talked at once, unobtrusively and with a bantering inconsequence that was never quite chatter, that was as cool as their white dresses and their impersonal eyes in the absence of all desire. They were here, and they accepted Tom and me, making only a polite pleasant effort to entertain or to be entertained. They knew that presently dinner would be over and a little later the evening too would be over and casually put away. It was sharply different from the West, where an evening was hurried from phase to phase towards its close, in a continually disappointed anticipation or else in sheer nervous dread of the moment itself.

'You make me feel uncivilized, Daisy,' I confessed on my second glass of corky but rather impressive claret. 'Can't you talk about crops or something?'

I meant nothing in particular by this remark, but it was taken up in an unexpected way.

'Civilization's going to pieces,' broke out Tom violently. 'I've gotten to be a terrible pessimist about things. Have you read *The Rise of the Coloured Empires* by this man Goddard?'

'Why, no,' I answered, rather surprised by his tone.

'Well, it's a fine book, and everybody ought to read it. The idea is if we don't look out the white race will be – will be utterly submerged. It's all scientific stuff; it's been proved.'

'Tom's getting very profound,' said Daisy, with an expression of unthoughtful sadness. 'He reads deep books with long words in them. What was that word we –'

CONTEXT

F. Scott Fitzgerald seems to be alluding to *The Rising Tide of Color Against White World Supremacy*, a racist account of contemporary history published in 1920 by Lothrop Stoddard (1883–1950).

'Well, these books are all scientific,' insisted Tom, glancing at her impatiently. 'This fellow has worked out the whole thing. It's up to us, who are the dominant race, to watch out or these other races will have control of things.'

'We've got to beat them down,' whispered Daisy, winking ferociously toward the fervent sun.

'You ought to live in California –' began Miss Baker, but Tom interrupted her by shifting heavily in his chair.

'This idea is that we're Nordics. I am, and you are, and you are, and –' After an infinitesimal hesitation he included Daisy with a slight nod, and she winked at me again. '– And we've produced all the things that go to make civilization – oh, science and art, and all that. Do you see?'

WWW. **CHECK THE NET**
http://www.
spiritone.com/
~gdy52150/1920s.
htm has a suitably
pointed exposition
of the rise of
American fascism
during the 1920s.

Reading this passage in isolation, it is easy to forget the important fact that *The Great Gatsby* is first of all a book about a man writing a book. We are not witnessing this scene at first hand, although it seems superficially as if we are. Nick Carraway is recreating events for us, filtering them through his own sense of their significance, and colouring them with hindsight.

F. Scott Fitzgerald, the real author of Nick's account, is presenting a scene, set within the Buchanans' house, and involving dramatic dialogue. One consequence of this method of narration is that it adds variety to the account. F. Scott Fitzgerald prevents his book becoming too introspective, too exclusively contained by Nick's own voice. Other voices enter here, assisting characterisation and developing the storyline.

Although the scene from which this extract is taken seems complete in itself, words and actions found here echo and foreshadow others throughout *The Great Gatsby*. This intricate patterning of the narrative, which can be extremely subtle, forms many threads of meaning which result in a rich and complex book, despite the fact that it is not a long novel.

Nick refers to Miss Baker. She will soon become Jordan, and before long he will be kissing her, but this is the first time they have met, so Nick indicates a degree of formality in their relationship at the time. Although she and Daisy discuss making a plan, Jordan is yawning, and Daisy is at a loss, unable to envisage a future that is different from the present. F. Scott Fitzgerald is portraying the lives of these rich Americans as lacking in purpose or direction. They merely drift, with the terrible sense that life holds no further possibilities for them.

CHECK THE NET
http://users.
snowcrest.net/
jmike/20sdep.html
has useful links
shedding light on
the lifestyle of the
leisured rich during
the 1920s and on
the sufferings of
the working class
during the decade
that followed.

Their conversation is neither expressive nor communicative, but consists of inconsequential banter, words uttered without any point. Nick notes 'the absence of all desire' (p. 17), indicating that these wealthy women have all they need and everything they want. Yet, in a sense they have nothing, for material possessions do not satisfy them; rather they are deadened by their wealth, as the phrase 'their impersonal eyes' (p. 17) suggests. That phrase contributes to one of the main thematic strands of the novel, which is concerned with sight and vision. At the beginning of the next chapter, those 'impersonal eyes' find an echo in the huge blank stare of Doctor T. J. Eckleburg.

Earlier in this opening chapter, Nick has spoken of Gatsby and his 'heightened sensitivity to the promises of life', his 'extraordinary gift for hope' (Chapter 1, p. 8). Nothing could be further from the ennui of the Buchanan household. Gatsby is driven by desire; for him life still has meaning and the future is alive with possibility. The contrast here should help us to understand the nature of that greatness which Nick discovered in Gatsby.

Instead of looking to the future and acting, Daisy focuses upon her injured finger. She is essentially a passive figure; things happen to her, and she is content to be shaped by events, rather than controlling her own destiny. She looks at the bruised finger 'with an awed expression' (p. 17). The adjective 'awed' seems entirely inappropriate to this trivial injury. It does add to our sense of Daisy's character in that it indicates a lack of proportion in her judgement and in her responses. She sees life in an exaggerated, distorted, ironical fashion. At the same time, 'awed' is an example of F. Scott Fitzgerald's careful verbal patterning as it anticipates the sense of wonder that informs Gatsby's enchanted vision.

The finger has been damaged by Tom, although Daisy admits it was an accident. The novel contains several further accidents, and many more allusions to the role of accidents in human life. The injury also foreshadows the incident in the next chapter, where Tom deliberately breaks the nose of his mistress, Myrtle Wilson. That brutal act is a violent response to the insistent repetition by Myrtle of Daisy's name. Here, Daisy upsets Tom by repeating the word 'hulking', and that parallel strengthens the foreshadowing, making the patterning of language and event more complex.

'Hulking' seems an appropriate word to describe Tom Buchanan, whose character is developed from an emphasis on his 'cruel body' (Chapter 1, p. 12). Tom presumably finds it objectionable because the word suggests a coarseness he associates with members of a lower social class than the one to which he proudly belongs.

Nick interrupts the dialogue to add a brief commentary on the distinction between social manners in the American East and the West. Significantly, dinner parties in the East are predictable and drift to an inevitable conclusion, whereas those in the West are agitated affairs, characterised by nervous energy, which may be uncomfortable, but at least have some vitality. Each phase of the Western dinner is a surge into the future, the anticipated moment, and although it is continually disappointed this forward motion is more alive than the Eastern drift.

It seems curious to talk in this way about a meal, but Nick is building a distinction that runs throughout the novel between the hopeful, forward-looking West, which is embodied in Gatsby, and the bored East, trapped in routine, with no desire to move beyond it.

Nick actually assumes the role of the unsophisticated rural Westerner, ironically requesting conversation about crops, with which he would feel more at home. Of course, he has been educated at Yale, and his casual remarks about the claret reveal his actual urbanity. We should not always take Nick at face value; he often lays claim to a simplicity that is clearly not truly his character.

Tom Buchanan also attended Yale. But the racist tirade which now follows indicates a boorishness that suggests he went to university

CHECK THE FILM
In the 1974 film version of *The Great Gatsby*, directed by Jack Clayton, Daisy was played by actress Mia Farrow. This casting emphasised Daisy's physical delicacy.

primarily to play football rather than to become educated. The manner, as well as the content, of his speech suggests philistinism and a basic lack of intelligence which conflicts with his characteristic air of social superiority. The crudity of his response to Goddard's book (which F. Scott Fitzgerald based upon an actual work published at the time) is given added emphasis by Daisy's remarks.

The fact that Daisy evidently does not like her husband, who has continually committed adultery since their marriage, makes her subsequent reluctance or inability to leave him still more striking. It emphasises the passivity which makes inevitable the failure of Gatsby's quest for her.

The women are dressed in white. Colour symbolism forms one of the main patterns in *The Great Gatsby*, and whiteness is one of its principal threads. F. Scott Fitzgerald uses its conventional connotations of purity and innocence, but here those familiar associations take on profoundly sinister significance as Tom violently proclaims the need to defend the superiority of the white race. Tom is presented as a foolish bigot, but the presentation of racial issues in the novel is far from straightforward.

CHECK THE BOOK

Jeffrey Louis Decker's essay 'Gatsby's Pristine Dream: The Diminishment of the Self-Made Man in the Tribal Twenties' (*Novel*, Fall 1994), pp. 52–71, sheds light on the nature of Tom Buchanan's racism.

F. Scott Fitzgerald was writing at a time when the composition of populations in American cities had been visibly altered by the continued flow of black Americans from the South, and by waves of immigration from southern and eastern Europe. Racial anxiety amongst the Anglo-Saxon elite was high, while amongst poorer 'Nordic' Americans (such as George Wilson) competition for jobs created genuine fears for survival. We have glimpses of these tensions in the novel (notably with the figure of Meyer Wolfshiem), but the action takes place largely within an elite world that was closed to the majority of Americans.

This is a novel of the Jazz Age, but one looks in vain for reference to Louis Armstrong, Bessie Smith, Fats Waller, Duke Ellington, Sidney Bechet and other leading practioners of this great African-American art form. Instead we are given Vladimir Tostoff's spurious concoction 'Jazz History of the World' (Chapter 3, p. 51). One suspects that F. Scott Fitzgerald was conscious of the irony here because *The Great Gatsby* is a novel of social criticism, and in this passage we find a concise portrayal of America divided along lines of class, gender and race.

TEXT 2 – PP. 56–8 (CHAPTER 3)

Reading over what I have written so far, I see I have given the impression that the events of three nights several weeks apart were all that absorbed me. On the contrary, they were merely casual events in a crowded summer, and, until much later, they absorbed me infinitely less than my personal affairs.

Most of the time I worked. In the early morning the sun threw my shadow westward as I hurried down the white chasms of lower New York to the Probity Trust. I knew the other clerks and young bond-salesmen by their first names, and lunched with them in dark, crowded restaurants on little pig sausages and mashed potatoes and coffee. I even had a short affair with a girl who lived in Jersey City and worked in the accounting department, but her brother began throwing mean looks in my direction, so when she went on her vacation in July I let it blow quietly away.

I took dinner usually at the Yale Club – for some reason it was the gloomiest event of my day – and then I went upstairs to the library and studied investments and securities for a conscientious hour. There were generally a few rioters around, but they never came into the library, so it was a good place to work. After that, if the night was mellow, I strolled down Madison Avenue past the old Murray Hill Hotel, and over 33rd Street to the Pennsylvania Station.

I began to like New York, the racy, adventurous feel of it at night, and the satisfaction that the constant flicker of men and women and machines gives to the restless eye. I liked to walk up Fifth Avenue and pick out romantic women from the crowd and imagine that in a few minutes I was going to enter into their lives, and no one would ever know or disapprove. Sometimes, in my mind, I followed them to their apartments on the corners of hidden streets, and they turned and smiled back at me before they faded through a door into warm darkness. At the enchanted metropolitan twilight I felt a haunting loneliness sometimes, and felt it in others – poor young clerks who loitered in front of windows waiting until it was time for a solitary restaurant dinner – young clerks in the dusk, wasting the most poignant moments of night and life.

CHECK THE BOOK

This 'constant flicker' echoes a phrase in Joseph Conrad's novella *Heart of Darkness* (written in 1899 and published in 1902), when Marlow, the narrator, contemplating 'very old times', says: 'We live in the flicker – may it last as long as the old earth keeps rolling!'

Again at eight o'clock, when the dark lanes of the Forties were lined five deep with throbbing taxicabs, bound for the theatre district, I felt a sinking in my heart. Forms leaned together in the taxis as they waited, and voices sang, and there was laughter from unheard jokes, and lighted cigarettes made unintelligible circles inside. Imagining that I, too, was hurrying towards gaiety and sharing their intimate excitement, I wished them well.

After a lengthy account of one of Gatsby's parties, Nick Carraway steps back to examine his telling of the story so far. In the process he reminds us of the fact that he is a writer as well as a narrator and that events which seem so immediate when we are caught up in the dialogue and description have actually been filtered through his recollection and reconstruction of them.

F. Scott Fitzgerald enriches his account and adds another level of meaning through this device of making Nick a character who is also author of this book. Of course, F. Scott Fitzgerald was the actual author. The Polish-born English novelist Joseph Conrad (1857–1924) used a comparable device in his novella *Heart of Darkness* (1902). F. Scott Fitzgerald was influenced by Conrad's example but added new dimensions when he created Nick Carraway.

> **? QUESTION**
> Discuss the reliability of Nick Carraway as the narrator of *The Great Gatsby*.

Nick casts a critical eye over his account and recognises that he has been misleading. Events that he describes as 'casual', meaning unexceptional or incidental, that at the time were less significant than many routine daily demands, have with hindsight come to seem central. That is the way they appear in his retrospective telling, and it confirms for us that he has become totally preoccupied with the life and death of Jay Gatsby.

What can we learn from that preoccupation? 'Most of the time I worked' (p. 56), Nick tells us. But his physical presence in New York's financial sector, selling bonds and reading up on securities and investments, is the mere surface of his own story. There is a turbulent inner life, a life of the imagination and of desire, which is revealed in this passage. Nick's company during the day is a group of unexceptional white-collar workers, dwarfed by the skyscrapers that form the city's 'white chasms'. They are on first-name terms and together they eat unexceptional food in dingy restaurants.

How different to the world created by Jay Gatsby, a man he cannot get to know in the same way he knows the clerks; 'The Great Gatsby', a lavish supplier of expensive food and drink to guests he himself scarcely knows.

Nick has a brief affair with a girl, until her brother scares him off. Why should Nick provoke 'mean looks' (p. 57)? He presents himself as decent and respectable and at the end of this chapter he declares, 'I am one of the few honest people that I have ever known' (Chapter 3, p. 59). Nick's self-proclaimed honesty is something readers should question. He may not consciously depart from telling the truth, as he sees it, but he has blind spots and seems to suppress or play down certain aspects of events to suit his own purposes.

He presents himself as a cool individual, who controls his emotions and leaves passion and desire to Jay Gatsby. The two men seem miles apart in temperament. But could it be that Gatsby embodies passion and desire that Nick feels and dare not give in to or even fully acknowledge? He discloses something of his emotional life here through his reference to 'romantic women' (p. 57) whom he pursues in his imagination, but the pursuit ends with a smile and a door closed against him. He is shut out from the 'warm darkness' of a mutually satisfying relationship.

Some of the most important literary figures of the early twentieth century were fascinated by the interior life of human beings and developed new ways of writing that traced the movements of the mind as it registered the events of the day, negligible as well as major, and as it responded to deep and often inexplicable impulses. One of these writers was the English novelist Virginia Woolf (1882–1941). In one of her best-known works, *Mrs Dalloway* (1925), exactly contemporary with *The Great Gatsby*, she created a character named Peter Walsh, who also dwells on loneliness and who follows a woman through the streets imagining himself a romantic buccaneer and colouring her too with his imaginings. *The Great Gatsby*, complex and concentrated though it is, is in most respects a more straightforward narrative than *Mrs Dalloway*, but both F. Scott Fitzgerald and Virginia Woolf were fascinated by the psychology of desire and found ways to represent it in literature.

> **? QUESTION**
> Are there grounds to support Nick's claim that he is honest? Are there grounds to doubt it?

CHECK THE NET

To read 'The Love Song of J. Alfred Prufrock', go to http://www.bartleby.com/198/1.html

Another contemporary literary character with whom Nick Carraway seems to have much in common at this point is J. Alfred Prufrock, who in T. S. Eliot's 'The Love Song of J. Alfred Prufrock' (1917) reveals himself as tormented by desire, susceptible to the sexual attractiveness of women yet unable to respond, too nervous or embarrassed to engage in the rituals of courtship. Nick presents himself as apprehensive that people might get to know about his romantic entanglements and disapprove of them. Yet towards the end of the next chapter Nick puts his arm around Jordan Baker's 'golden shoulder' (Chapter 4, p. 77), draws her towards him and invites her to dinner. There seems to be some inconsistency here. Is Nick being entirely honest with us?

The sentence 'Forms leaned together in the taxis as they waited, and voices sang, and there was laughter from unheard jokes, and lighted cigarettes made unintelligible circles inside' (pp. 57–8) is strikingly effective on account of its use of the conjunction 'and'. Simple statements are linked together simply by this conjunction. The effect is to convey what Nick sees and hears as a series of sense impressions, without further explanation. He is outside all this activity, not a part of it. This style of writing conveys that detachment and the word 'unintelligible' seals the impression he aims to convey of a lonely man, excluded from intimacy.

Nick avoids the riotous elements who frequent the Yale Club, yet he is drawn to the racy and adventurous feel of the New York City night. His character is not simple and self-evident. As a consequence of this, being honest is a far more complex matter than he admits. While Nick, despite his declared reticence, seems to have an affair with Jordan and mentions other girlfriends, the glamorous Jay Gatsby, who now preoccupies him, remains chastely devoted to an idealised woman, who certainly cannot be credibly identified with the flesh and blood Daisy Buchanan we are shown in Nick's account.

Nick refers to specific places in New York, the names of streets and buildings. He is discussing his personal life, his feelings and the flights of his imagination, yet he embeds all that subjective experience in a social world that actually exists and can be found on maps or visited by others. Throughout *The Great Gatsby* historically verifiable data is interwoven with the stuff of romance; the material world and an ideal world coexist both as thematic issues and in the way the novel is composed.

TEXT 3 – PP. 88–9 (CHAPTER 5)

We went upstairs, through period bedrooms swathed in rose and lavender silk and vivid with new flowers, through dressing-rooms and poolrooms, and bath-rooms with sunken baths – intruding into one chamber where a dishevelled man in pyjamas was doing liver exercises on the floor. It was Mr Klipspringer, the 'boarder'. I had seen him wandering hungrily about the beach that morning. Finally we came to Gatsby's own apartment, a bedroom and a bath, and an Adam's study, where we sat down and drank a glass of some Chartreuse he took from a cupboard in the wall.

He hadn't once ceased looking at Daisy, and I think he revalued everything in the house according to the measure of response it drew from her well-loved eyes. Sometimes too, he stared around at his possessions in a dazed way, as though in her actual and astounding presence none of it was any longer real. Once he nearly toppled down a flight of stairs.

His bedroom was the simplest room of all – except where the dresser was garnished with a toilet set of pure dull gold. Daisy took the brush with delight, and smoothed her hair, whereupon Gatsby sat down and shaded his eyes and began to laugh.

'It's the funniest thing, old sport,' he said hilariously. 'I can't – When I try to – '

He had passed visibly through two states and was entering upon a third. After his embarrassment and his unreasoning joy he was consumed with wonder at her presence. He had been full of the idea so long, dreamed it right through to the end, waited with his teeth set, so to speak, at an inconceivable pitch of intensity. Now, in the reaction, he was running down like an over-wound clock.

Recovering himself in a minute he opened for us two hulking patent cabinets which held his massed suits and dressing-gowns and ties, and his shirts, piled like bricks in stacks a dozen high.

CHECK THE NET

The liqueur Chartreuse is a rich green colour which fits into the book's scheme of significant colours; it is also a drink with connections to the European Middle Ages. See http://www. chartreuse.fr/ pa_history_uk.htm

'I've got a man in England who buys me clothes. He sends over a selection of things at the beginning of each season, spring and fall.'

He took out a pile of shirts and began throwing them, one by one, before us, shirts of sheer linen and thick silk and fine flannel, which lost their folds as they fell and covered the table in many coloured disarray. While we admired he brought more and the soft rich heap mounted higher – shirts with stripes and scrolls and plaids in coral and apple-green and lavender and faint orange, with monograms of indian blue. Suddenly, with a strained sound, Daisy bent her head into the shirts and began to cry stormily.

'They're such beautiful shirts,' she sobbed, her voice muffled in the thick folds. 'It makes me sad because I've never seen such – such beautiful shirts before.'

The episode in which Gatsby and Daisy are reunited in his mansion is clearly a highly significant one. It is an encounter that carries an enormous amount of weight in the novel, and, after disclosing to us that Daisy falls terribly short of the ideal version lodged in Gatsby's heart and imagination, F. Scott Fitzgerald has to ensure that the two figures do not appear simply ridiculous.

It might seem obvious that Gatsby and Daisy have a lot of catching up to do, and would feel the need to talk at length. But although F. Scott Fitzgerald is extremely skilled as a writer of dialogue he wisely opts to keep their conversation to a minimum. Their feelings for one another are communicated through their actions and through what remains unsaid.

 CHECK THE NET

http://www. greentequila.com/ apexperts/ earlytwentieth/ performing/ drama.html#belasco
places Belasco in the context of American drama between 1900 and 1950.

The description of the interior of Gatsby's mansion is highly economical yet it conveys both opulence and meticulous stage management. In Chapter 3, in the library, Owl Eyes compares Gatsby to the theatrical director David Belasco (1853–1931), renowned for the painstaking realism of his stagecraft. The mansion is not a home but an extravagant prop in Gatsby's dramatic representation of his love and desire. It is a drama he has designed for a single onlooker, Daisy Buchanan née Fay, and now she is herself a participant in the spectacle.

Colours are beautifully coordinated; fabrics have been selected with impeccable care, presumably not by the house's owner, who simply pays for such services, allowing an Englishman to buy his clothes in accordance with the latest exclusive fashions.

Ewing Klipspringer is described as a 'boarder' (p. 88). His actual status within the household is shadowy, but he is pressed to play the piano for Gatsby and Daisy. In effect he is another prop. There is certainly no trace of real friendship between him and his host; after Gatsby's death Klipspringer is more interested in retrieving his shoes than attending the funeral. He is interrupted doing exercises to stimulate his liver, a necessary regimen in a social circle where heavy drinking prevails.

Gatsby has a study, although there is no indication that he has at any time in his adult life been a studious man. The room is integral to the aristocratic image cultivated through the mansion as a whole. It is said to be in the classical architectural style of eighteenth-century brothers Robert Adam (1728–92) and James Adam (1730–94). The real name Adam adds one more historical detail, but it also fits into F. Scott Fitzgerald's intricate patterning of language, evoking Adam the first man, in the Garden of Eden, and his temptation by Eve.

Gatsby and his guests drink Chartreuse, a bright green liqueur. Its greenness conforms to the novel's careful patterning of colour, and green carries obvious associations of the natural world. In the early years of America's settlement by Europeans, the New World was repeatedly compared to a garden, and to the Garden of Eden in particular. It is through such attention to detail that F. Scott Fitzgerald manages to condense so much meaning into his relatively short novel. It is **ironic** that green is here associated with alcohol. Gatsby is an ostensibly Adamic figure who is actually a bootlegger. When Nick says that Gatsby at one point nearly falls down the stairs he is showing a man intoxicated with love.

At the core of this man's adult passion is an adolescent fixation. It was a teenage boy who became obsessed with Daisy Fay and despite intervening years of experience, and his affairs in the past with other women, we see awkwardness and embarrassment in Gatsby's

CHECK THE BOOK

R. W. B. Lewis's *The American Adam: Innocence, Tragedy, and Tradition in the Nineteenth Century* (University of Chicago Press, 1955) is a classic study of the recurrence of the biblical figure of Adam as a thematic touchstone in nineteenth-century American literature. Lewis shows that Gatsby, F. Scott Fitzgerald's deeply ironic Adam, had numerous precursors in American writing.

behaviour at this point that seems more in keeping with the reaction of an inexperienced youth. The intensity of his feelings is stressed as Gatsby sinks into inarticulacy, overcome by the seductiveness of Daisy brushing her hair. He falls back upon his prop cupboard, piling up shirts as though they were a measure of his feelings. Daisy collapses in a flood of tears.

Words are inadequate to express what Gatsby feels for Daisy, and words fail to cope with the complexity of her emotional response to him. Unable to say directly what they feel they seize on other options: Gatsby falls silent, then talks of other things; Daisy cries. F. Scott Fitzgerald recognised that putting expressions of love directly into the mouths of these characters would have produced a sense of anticlimax. By showing their inability to speak he implies a great deal going on beneath the surface. Gatsby's 'old sport' is a verbal mannerism that stands in much the same relation to his underlying emotions as the pristine shirt he wears does to the beating of his heart.

Gatsby is compared to 'an over-wound clock' (p. 89). It is an image that may recall the clock ticking by his bedside during his teenage years as he imagined his new self into existence, but it fits more generally into the novel's complicated treatment of time. The key point is that Gatsby envisages his future in terms of an event that is irretrievably in the past. He envisages a future time when he can live perpetually in the intensity of that moment when he fell in love with Daisy.

F. Scott Fitzgerald suggests a parallel between that self-deluding obsession and a sense of past, present and future that has been evident in American culture more generally. The ideal American future has been cast frequently as a return to Eden, a radiant world that ceased to exist before human history could even begin. There was no sense of time in the Garden; it was only loss of Eden that made awareness of the future possible for human beings. The intense present that Gatsby longs for is an impossible dream. The final words of the novel compare human beings to boats struggling against the current, 'borne back ceaselessly into the past' (Chapter 9, p. 172). However strong our desire, we cannot arrest the inexorable passage of time.

CHECK THE BOOK

In 1925 the poet William Carlos Williams (1883–1963) published *In the American Grain*, a prose work that explores the mingling of myth and reality in the stories surrounding key figures in America's history. As an alternative way of writing history it is an illuminating book to read alongside *The Great Gatsby*.

TEXT 4 – PP. 94–6 (CHAPTER 6)

James Gatz – that was really, or at least legally, his name. He had changed it at the age of seventeen and at the specific moment that witnessed the beginning of his career – when he saw Dan Cody's yacht drop anchor over the most insidious flat on Lake Superior. It was James Gatz who had been loafing along the beach that afternoon in a torn green jersey and a pair of canvas pants, but it was already Jay Gatsby who borrowed a rowboat, pulled out to the *Tuolomee*, and informed Cody that a wind might catch him and break him up in half an hour.

I suppose he'd had the name ready for a long time, even then. His parents were shiftless and unsuccessful farm people – his imagination had never really accepted them as his parents at all. The truth was that Jay Gatsby of West Egg, Long Island, sprang from his Platonic conception of himself. He was a son of God – a phrase which, if it means anything, means just that – and he must be about His Father's business, the service of a vast, vulgar, and meretricious beauty. So he invented just the sort of Jay Gatsby that a seventeen-year-old boy would be likely to invent, and to this conception he was faithful to the end.

For over a year he had been beating his way along the south shore of Lake Superior as a clam-digger and a salmon-fisher or in any other capacity that brought him food and bed. His brown, hardening body lived naturally through the half-fierce, half-lazy work of the bracing days. He knew women early, and since they spoiled him he became contemptuous of them, of young virgins because they were ignorant, of the others because they were hysterical about things which in his overwhelming self-absorption he took for granted.

But his heart was in a constant, turbulent riot. The most grotesque and fantastic conceits haunted him in his bed at night. A universe of ineffable gaudiness spun itself out in his brain while the clock ticked on the washstand and the moon soaked with wet light his tangled clothes upon the floor. Each night he added to the pattern of his fancies until drowsiness closed down upon some vivid scene with an oblivious embrace. For a while

www. CHECK THE NET
See http://www.sc.edu/fitzgerald/collection/dustjackets/gatsby.html for a reproduction of Francis Cugat's original dust jacket illustration for *The Great Gatsby*.

these reveries provided an outlet for his imagination; they were a satisfactory hint of the unreality of reality, a promise that the rock of the world was founded securely on a fairy's wing.

An instinct toward his future glory had led him, some months before, to the small Lutheran college of St Olaf's in southern Minnesota. He stayed there two weeks, dismayed at its ferocious indifference to the drums of his destiny, to destiny itself, and despising the janitor's work with which he was to pay his way through. Then he drifted back to Lake Superior, and he was still searching for something to do on the day that Dan Cody's yacht dropped anchor in the shallows alongshore.

This passage from Chapter 6 shows Nick Carraway piecing together Gatsby's past, penetrating the mystery that has surrounded the man to reveal an act of self-creation that Nick sees as heroic, even if doomed to failure.

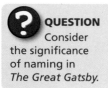

QUESTION
Consider the significance of naming in *The Great Gatsby*.

Gatsby's legal name is James Gatz but, as we discover, the law is for him a lesser reality than his own vision. A name change has major significance for Gatsby, because he believes it is the key to changing his self. In effect, he is like a magician using the power of words to transform one object into something else, something of far greater value. Gatz is a solid, unglamorous, monosyllabic name. He must shed it, just as he leaves behind the casual beach clothes he wore as a boy, and put on a new name, Gatsby, the verbal equivalent to his expensive silk shirts. The name is the cornerstone of his new image.

Nick tells how Gatsby is transfixed by Dan Cody's yacht, just as he is later transfixed by Daisy Fay. (Daisy changes her name, under law, in marriage, and it is part of Gatsby's plan to reverse that change.) The yacht's glamour affects him as a glimpse into a previously unknown world, which he now feels he must enter. The name of Lake Superior, while a realistic geographical detail, seems to carry symbolic value that seals his fate. Gatz must become Gatsby and enter this superior realm.

James Gatz is presented as a kind of noble savage, living off the land and with intimate understanding of it, like a Native American tribesman, or a Frontier scout living by his wits. The primitive simplicity of his existence is in stark contrast to the extravagant lifestyle he will later cultivate, and the evident health of his hard, brown body will be superseded by a moral sickness or corruption unconvincingly concealed beneath expensive suits. In the presentation of the boy, F. Scott Fitzgerald is giving us an inhabitant of the **mythical** West, uncorrupted by the sophistication of the East's Europeanised lifestyle.

His parents are farm people, conforming to Thomas Jefferson's agrarian ideal. However, they are not figures from an ideal world, but farmers in historical America, and they are classified not only as 'unsuccessful', indicating failure in material terms, but also as 'shiftless' (p. 95) suggesting their flawed character as human beings and their lack of purpose or drive.

At seventeen, in transition from childhood to maturity, James Gatz decides to reject his parents. In this, he might be seen to parallel America, which in 1776 threw off the rule of Europe with its paternalistic monarchs. Moreover, he springs from 'his Platonic conception of himself' (p. 95). F. Scott Fitzgerald is not suggesting that the boy has read the Greek philosopher, but that he has an ideal conception of who he is, which is in accord with Plato's belief that true reality lies in an ideal realm, beyond the material world that we encounter daily through our senses. Gatz believes that he can transcend the limitations of his material circumstances, and create himself anew. F. Scott Fitzgerald is implying that this parallels the faith upon which America was created as a modern democratic nation.

The Great Gatsby makes it clear that America has in some respects failed in this aspiration, as the persistent imitation of European models suggests. The ideal American republic was an egalitarian democracy, but the America depicted in this novel seems closer in that respect to Plato's ideal republic, which was rigidly stratified into classes. Plato argued that social class was based in the composition of the soul. His aristocracy had souls which he compared to gold. They were served by a warrior class, whose souls he compared to silver. The working class were bronze. It was impossible in Plato's republic for a member of the lower class to

> **CONTEXT**
>
> In the eighteenth century, around the time America came into existence, there was a fashion for the notion of the 'noble savage', the idea – largely derived from the philosopher Jean-Jacques Rousseau (1712–78) – that before the acquisition of private property human beings lived peacefully and harmoniously, in accordance with their innate nobility. James Gatz is cast in this light.

cross into the golden realm of the aristocracy. In twentieth-century America, James Gatz is trying to make just that transition.

F. Scott Fitzgerald alludes not only to Platonic idealism, but also to Judaeo-Christian faith in an order of reality beyond the material world. Gatz is described as a 'son of God' (p. 95), which appears to allude to Christ, whose words reported in Luke's gospel (2:49) concerning the need to be about His Father's business are echoed here.

CHECK THE BOOK

Susan Strasser's book *Satisfaction Guaranteed: The Making of the American Mass Market*, (Pantheon, 1989) is a lively account of the history of advertising in modern America. It shows that as mass production took hold, the emphasis in advertising changed from the basic service of informing potential buyers what was available to techniques of active persuasion, designed with increasing subtlety to convince Americans of their need to buy certain consumer items.

To cast Gatsby as Christ would be a provocative gesture. But remember that the vision of the divine we see in this novel is George Wilson's mistaken identification of the advertising hoarding as God. If advertising is America's god in the 1920s, then Gatsby might more credibly be held to be his son.

The story of Christ does provide an example of sacrifice leading to redemption. It is tempting to suggest that Nick is presenting his writing of Gatsby's story as a kind of resurrection in which Gatsby returns to life in art. As 'The Great Gatsby', in Nick's account, the man embodies a vision that might redeem a world which has drifted into indifference and the conviction of its own futility.

Adam also was a son of God, and it is easier to draw a parallel with this primal figure, the new man in the new world. It was a familiar convention in nineteenth-century American literature to compare the American in the New World to Adam in Eden. The Adamic qualities of innocence and clear-sightedness scarcely apply to James Gatz, whose sexual adventures begin early and whose vision is troubled by 'grotesque and fantastic conceits' (p. 95), but they might be attributed to Jay Gatsby, as he begins the world again within his imagination.

Note that F. Scott Fitzgerald uses the word 'invent'. This gives a practical aspect to the self-creation, making Gatsby an inventor in a country which has taken pride in invention, from Benjamin Franklin (who is later invoked in James Gatz's Schedule) to F. Scott Fitzgerald's contemporary, Thomas Edison.

America has not really managed to break with the past. This novel's insistent reference to the fact that Americans were drawn into the First World War is a clear example of the nation's inability to stand outside of history. Similarly, Gatsby has not really escaped from his past; he has not managed to transcend the material circumstances of life in twentieth-century America. So, as Nick comments, he serves 'a vast, vulgar, and meretricious beauty' (p. 95).

This phrase describes well the gaudy commercialism of life in America as F. Scott Fitzgerald knew it. The word 'meretricious' means 'showily attractive', and carries associations of prostitution. It is an example of the difficult or obscure vocabulary which F. Scott Fitzgerald occasionally attributes to his narrator, Nick Carraway. Such words mark the narrator as an educated man, with literary aspirations. They also appeal to a certain level of sophistication in his readers.

The reference to a ticking clock draws us into the novel's complex handling of time. Here, the mechanical movement of a clock's hands seems to belong to a world quite distinct from the turbulent inner life of James Gatz. His imagination appears to operate according to another system of time altogether. The power of his fantasies convinces him that the reality of the world around him is actually unreal. As Nick puts it, 'the rock of the world was founded securely on a fairy's wing' (p. 96). This seems to contain an allusion to Daisy, whose original surname, Fay, is an old English word for 'fairy'. More generally, it suggests that the material world is dependent upon an ideal world, and that the magical touch of the ideal can transform material reality. The truth is that Gatsby remains in a world of clocks that continue to tick, while other machines, such as cars and guns, determine his fate. So what value is there in his romantic vision of an enchanted world?

One answer seems to reside in the concluding paragraph of this passage where we are made aware in more mundane terms of Gatsby's dissatisfaction with the hand life has dealt him. Unlike the other characters in the novel, caught in their routine lives, he has the energy and the vision to lift himself out of his allotted role. The new role may ultimately prove inadequate, but the energy and the vision that drive him are offered for our admiration.

In this concluding paragraph, F. Scott Fitzgerald uses the phrase 'ferocious indifference' (p. 96). In **Text 1** we saw Daisy 'winking

www. CHECK THE NET
The American declaration of war is reproduced at http://www. flrstworldwar.com/ source/usofficial awardeclaration.htm

ferociously' (Chapter 1, p. 18). These are good examples of a stylistic device used on numerous occasions in the novel. An adjective (or adverb) is coupled with a noun (or verb) which it seems to contradict, creating in effect an **oxymoron**. The surprise of such combinations forces us to pause in reading, and to consider the implications for our interpretation of such apparent contradiction. Here, the sense of ferocity lurking beneath the veneer of polite society may indicate an underlying savagery within this civilised society. It may also register the intensity of Gatsby's reaction to a world that seems restrictive in its very ordinariness.

TEXT 5 – PP. 170–2 (CHAPTER 9)

Gatsby's house was still empty when I left – the grass on his lawn had grown as long as mine. One of the taxi drivers in the village never took a fare past the entrance gate without stopping for a minute and pointing inside; perhaps it was he who drove Daisy and Gatsby over to East Egg the night of the accident, and perhaps he had made a story about it all his own. I didn't want to hear it and I avoided him when I got off the train.

I spent my Saturday nights in New York because those gleaming, dazzling parties of his were with me so vividly that I still could hear the music and the laughter, faint and incessant, from his garden, and the cars going up and down his drive. One night I did hear a material car there, and saw its lights stop at his front steps. But I didn't investigate. Probably it was some final guest who had been away at the ends of the earth and didn't know that the party was over.

On the last night, with my trunk packed and my car sold to the grocer, I went over and looked at that huge incoherent failure of a house once more. On the white steps an obscene word, scrawled by some boy with a piece of brick, stood out clearly in the moonlight, and I erased it, drawing my shoe raspingly along the stone. Then I wandered down to the beach and sprawled out on the sand.

Most of the big shore places were closed now and there were hardly any lights except the shadowy, moving glow of a ferryboat across the Sound. And as the moon rose higher the inessential houses began to melt away until gradually I became aware of the old island here that flowered once for Dutch sailors' eyes – a fresh, green breast of the new world. Its vanished trees, the trees that had made way for Gatsby's house, had once pandered in whispers to the last and greatest of all human dreams; for a transitory enchanted moment man must have held his breath in the presence of this continent, compelled into an aesthetic contemplation he neither understood nor desired, face to face for the last time in history with something commensurate to his capacity for wonder.

And as I sat there brooding on the old, unknown world, I thought of Gatsby's wonder when he first picked out the green light at the end of Daisy's dock. He had come a long way to this blue lawn, and his dream must have seemed so close that he could hardly fail to grasp it. He did not know that it was already behind him, somewhere back in that vast obscurity beyond the city, where the dark fields of the republic rolled on under the night.

Gatsby believed in the green light, the orgastic future that year by year recedes before us. It eluded us then, but that's no matter – tomorrow we will run faster, stretch out our arms further … And one fine morning –

So we beat on, boats against the current, borne back ceaselessly into the past.

The concluding pages of *The Great Gatsby* are justly famous. Initially, F. Scott Fitzgerald placed the reference to the Dutch sailors at the end of Chapter 1, but in the course of writing the book he shifted it to the end, where it provides a suitably evocative conclusion to a novel that is remarkably rich in meaning.

The word 'last' recurs in this passage, which has an air of finality throughout. The party is over in a literal and a **metaphorical** sense, and Nick is preparing to leave the East for the Midwest. It is as if his own life has ceased with Gatsby's death, and two years after returning home he will write this account, living the experiences again in the composition of his book. We do not know what happens to him in the intervening period, but the impression is that Nick's life has in effect been suspended.

The passage of time is indicated through the growth of the grass on Gatsby's lawn. This image of natural growth draws attention to the

www. CHECK THE NET

See http://www.pbs.org/wgbh/aia/part1/1h289.html. It is thought-provoking to contrast this idealised image of Dutch sailors encountering the New World with the image shown on this web page of enslaved Africans, captured from a Spanish vessel, being landed at Jamestown, Virginia, in 1619 by Dutch sailors.

TEXT 5 – PP. 170–2 (CHAPTER 9) continued

www. CHECK THE NET
http://memory.loc.gov/ammem/coolhtml/coolhome.html is an excellent resource for exploring America's consumer culture of the 1920s.

artifice involved in keeping the lawn neat, in conformity with Gatsby's image. He was not really Adam in Eden, but a rich man with servants to trim the grass. The material perfection he strove for was distant from the lushness and vitality that F. Scott Fitzgerald refers to in this passage as the 'fresh, green breast of the new world' (p. 171).

Nick's reference to the taxi driver who acts as a kind of grotesque tourist guide reminds us that this is a society that loves a spectacle, especially if tinged with scandal. Myrtle Wilson loved to read gossipy stories in *Town Tattle*, and such magazines were immensely popular in America in the 1920s.

Nick speculates that the driver may have made a story of his own to explain events. This is in fact the procedure that most of the characters in this novel are involved in, including Nick himself. They are weaving stories around the objects and events in their world in order to make sense of them, and because he cultivated mystery, Gatsby provided a singularly rich focus for speculation and invention. He continues to do so after his death.

Nick is sensitive to the memory of his neighbour, and avoids hearing further fabrications. Still, he is haunted by his memory, and writes his book in order to preserve the value he perceived in Gatsby. There is an intriguing parallel between Gatsby's obsession with Daisy, including his rapt contemplation of the green light, which he associates with her, and the obsession that leads Nick to produce his account of the man he contemplates as 'The Great Gatsby'. In both cases we might consider the object of the obsession to be unworthy of the attention and of the energy expended. But Nick points out earlier in the novel that Gatsby's vision goes far beyond Daisy, and we might conclude that Nick's own vision, contained in his book, goes beyond the flawed individual who owns the mansion next door.

His engagement with the past is vividly rendered in this passage through the strength of his imagination summoning up the parties, in both visual and auditory terms. The house now stands empty, like an abandoned film set. Mention of 'a material car' (p. 170) picks up on the recurrent thematic distinction between 'materialism' and 'idealism' as two distinct versions of reality.

Nick has sold his own car to the grocer. It is a modest vehicle, which a tradesman can afford, unlike the expensive vehicles owned by Gatsby. His imminent departure for the Midwest returns us to the theme of distinctions between America's East and West which is one of the major threads running through the novel.

Another prominent theme is evident in Nick's perception of Gatsby's house as a 'huge incoherent failure' (p. 171). The use of 'incoherent' to describe a house is an instance of F. Scott Fitzgerald's bold use of apparently inappropriate adjectives. Despite its ostensible status as an index of material success, the mansion is actually a measure of failure in terms of democratic ideals. Like its owner it is magnificent yet flawed, and ultimately it does not hold together.

The moonlight seems to carry us into the domain of **romance**, which Nathaniel Hawthorne had described so helpfully in his preface to *The Scarlet Letter* (1850). But initially, instead of creating an enchanted space, the moon illuminates an obscene word written on a step by a boy. Gatsby's effort at self-creation began with a word, the changing of his name. Here we encounter a word that has no power to transform, but instead confronts us with a harsh and unpleasant reality. The fact that it was a boy who scrawled the obscenity undermines any romantic notion we may retain that childhood is a time of innocence. Corruption has already entered the life of this child, growing up in modern America. Nick, a writer sensitive to words and their power, erases the obscenity. He wants his carefully chosen and organised language to delineate Jay Gatsby for posterity, not this arbitrary and offensive scrawl.

Nick goes to the beach, to the edge of the continent. Here the rising moon does, finally, cast the light of romance mentioned by Nathaniel Hawthorne, and in the enchanted space it creates Nick has a vision that transcends the moment and carries him back to the arrival on this coast centuries before of pioneering Dutch sailors. The lush vegetation that greeted them has gone now, but the memory of America as **Utopia**, the projection of human dreams and aspirations, is preserved in Nick's culminating romantic vision.

The sailors sensed that this land would allow the return of a Golden Age. That sense of unlimited potential fuelled the vision of

> **CONTEXT**
>
> Sir Thomas More (1478–1535) published *Utopia* (1516), which became a famous account of an imagined social order. Some idealistic Americans have sought to match in reality such literary flights of imagination and have established 'utopian' communities.

the New World that lured countless immigrants from the Old World to its shores. But the complicated treatment of time that concludes this passage and ends the book indicates that the return to paradise that was envisaged by these settlers was always an ideal rather than a material reality. That vision of America was utopian and belonged to the Golden Age that Plato projected not into the future but into the past. It was a myth, and the inexorable trend of human history has been to move away from the ideal, more deeply into the material world.

Gatsby believed in the 'orgastic future' (p. 171). His goal was a life of ecstatic intensity, of continuous exhilarating *becoming* rather than dull routine *being*. Nick recognised the value of this aspiration in the context of New York's purposeless drift and that of the modern world more generally. We saw Gatsby with arms outstretched at the end of Chapter 1. Now, at the end of the book, we find another memorable image of outstretched arms, an image of human desire striving for some vital, yet unspecified, goal.

CHECK THE BOOK

The distinction between *being* and *becoming* is of vital importance to Amory Blaine, protagonist of F. Scott Fitzgerald's first novel, *This Side of Paradise*.

CRITICAL APPROACHES

THEMES

AMERICAN IDEALS

The American literary critic Lionel Trilling (1905–75) argued that, in a sense, Gatsby *is* America, and it is certainly the case that an overarching concern of the novel is the condition of America in the early twentieth century. More specifically, F. Scott Fitzgerald is examining the fate of American ideals during a period when the aspirations expressed in the Declaration of Independence, issued in 1776, were under threat from the pressures of modern life. His favoured title for the book was, after all, *Under the Red, White, and Blue*, invoking the Stars and Stripes, the national flag, as an emblem of those ideals.

Thomas Jefferson and the Founding Fathers who formulated the Declaration enshrined within it fundamental equalities in American life. Yet F. Scott Fitzgerald depicts a society that is riven by class distinctions, dramatically rendered in the different fortunes of Tom Buchanan, residing in fashionable East Egg, and George Wilson, trapped in the dismal 'valley of ashes' (Chapter 2, p. 26). The conception of America nurtured by Jefferson was of an agrarian society living from the land; but the census of 1920 showed that statistically America had become a predominantly urban nation for the first time. Also, America was to be in the Jeffersonian conception a peace-loving nation, escaping the ruinous conflicts that characterised European history. F. Scott Fitzgerald stresses the significance to his characters of the First World War (1914–18), where America was drawn in April 1917 into just such a disastrous and wasteful European conflict.

America has traditionally cherished the notion of the self-determining individual, living with minimal interference or regulation from government or social pressures. Thomas Jefferson (1743–1826), who became America's third president, argued 'That government is best which governs least', and in the nineteenth century the New England philosopher Henry David Thoreau

CONTEXT

John Dos Passos (1896–1970), one of the major novelists amongst F. Scott Fitzgerald's contemporaries, was disturbed by what he saw as twentieth-century America's abandonment of its fundamental values and founding ideals. His brilliant novel *Manhattan Transfer* (1925) depicts a society where a vast gap has opened between rich and poor and where narrow selfishness and materialism prevail.

CONTEXT

Thomas Jefferson (1743–1826) became the third president of the United States (1801–09). He was a remarkable man but like many of his contemporaries amongst the American ruling class he was a slave owner. His advocacy of equal rights for all turned a blind eye to those he held in slavery, and his preference for an agrarian economy was similarly blinkered with respect to slaves who worked the land.

AMERICAN IDEALS continued

(1817–62) went further, suggesting 'That government is best which governs not at all'. *The Great Gatsby* portrays a society in which individuals have been regimented during wartime, and subjected to Prohibition laws during peacetime. We are told that as a young officer, Jay Gatsby 'was liable at the whim of an impersonal government to be blown anywhere about the world' (Chapter 8, p. 142). More generally the novel shows the emergence of a mass society with pressure placed upon individual integrity from such sources as advertising and fashion, through images spread by cinema and magazines.

The concept of the self-regulating individual must be revised in a society where you are what you wear, and where you are defined by the car you drive or the house in which you live. F. Scott Fitzgerald draws a sharp contrast between the Gatsby image that is presented to Daisy across the bay, and the self-sufficient adolescent, James Gatz, whose body grew hard and brown as he roamed the shore of Lake Superior.

www. CHECK THE NET
For information on Lake Superior visit **http://www. eagleharborcam.com /lakesuperiorinfo. html**

The relationship between the Old World and the New provided the crucial material in the fiction of Henry James (1843–1916), a major figure in the literary generation preceding that to which F. Scott Fitzgerald belonged. James called this relationship the 'international theme'. F. Scott Fitzgerald's meditation on American history and American ideals also uses cross-cultural comparison. Throughout the novel a recurrent theme is the importation of European fashions, manners and habits into the American context, invariably to the detriment of American ways.

The famous concluding vision of the Dutch sailors, encountering with wonder 'a fresh, green breast of the new world' (Chapter 9, p. 171) evokes an ideal America which has been perpetuated in American culture. As settlers pushed further into the continent, heading westward, the notion of a new start was continually revived. The Frontier has remained a powerful term in evoking entry into the unknown and the adventure of starting afresh.

In reality, the Frontier marking the limit of westward settlement of the American continent was exhausted by the end of the nineteenth century. Americans have had to find other ways of pushing back the Frontier, including space travel.

THE AMERICAN DREAM

F. Scott Fitzgerald exploits the tensions that exist between two variant definitions of the American Dream. The first is an ideal version, which preserves the sense of wonder and limitless possibility at the heart of what America means. This America is an embodiment of human potential, free from any limits set by past experience. It is this aspect of Jay Gatsby that Nick Carraway admires unequivocally.

Another version of the American Dream has come to be predominant, however. This is a materialistic version in which the process of creating one's self is equated with getting rich. The acquisition of wealth allows certain material freedoms and possibilities that remain forever closed to the poor. The rags-to-riches story, popularised in the works of Horatio Alger (1832–99), has come to be more closely identified with the notion of the American Dream than the alternative, idealistic vision. It is the corrupt means by which Gatsby has achieved wealth and his vulgar exhibitions of affluence that provoke Nick's scorn.

Gatsby has recreated himself, shedding the past, abandoning his parents, just as America tried to jettison European history and Old World values with its Declaration of Independence in 1776. Gatsby's desire was to create an ideal self, held together by hope and wonder. But this ideal is tainted by the criminal means he employed to attain his evident wealth. In terms of F. Scott Fitzgerald's symbolism, the New World's 'green breast' (p. 171), living and nourishing, has diminished to become the 'green light' at the end of the Buchanans' dock, the artificial marker of a rich man's property.

The tension here may be formulated in terms of *success* and *failure*, which are clearly thematic issues of concern to F. Scott Fitzgerald. He presents an apparent **paradox** in which success in material terms – the acquisition of the trappings of wealth – inescapably means failure in terms of the ideal.

Yet it is not just the rich who sacrifice their individuality and their freedom in order to acquire money and property. George Wilson is unequivocally a failure, in economic terms and as a husband to

> **CONTEXT**
>
> Horatio Alger (1832–99) wrote more than one hundred books arguing that religious belief and hard work could enable any young American to secure material advancement and success. F. Scott Fitzgerald portrays such faith in industriousness and diligence as illusory. Inheritance and crime are the principal routes to wealth and status in *The Great Gatsby*. The American writer Nathanael West (1903–40) satirised the Alger stories in his curious novella *A Cool Million* (1934), where a young man named Lemuel Pitkin, seeking advancement through honest means, is repeatedly cheated and in the end is physically mutilated.

CONTEXT

The American writer William Dean Howells (1837–1920) had earlier addressed these issues of material success and moral failure in his novel *The Rise of Silas Lapham* (1885), where a paint manufacturer, caught up in the cut and thrust of business, loses his sensitivity to other people's needs and feelings as he gains material wealth.

CHECK THE BOOK

Henry Nash Smith's *Virgin Land: The American West as Symbol and Myth* (Harvard University Press, 1971) is a fascinating study of the significance of the West within America's perception of itself. It contains sections on Thomas Jefferson and his ideals, the popularisation of the frontiersman as Western hero, utopian agrarianism and the myth of the New World garden, and the Frontier thesis offered by historian Frederick Jackson Turner.

Myrtle. He has few possessions, but he is ensnared as a worker, a drudge within the economic system, with no room to manoeuvre. His dream, expressed to Tom, who is alarmed at the prospect, is to go West with his wife, and to begin life anew; but it is just a dream and one that will not be realised.

THE FRONTIER

Early settlers from Europe spoke of the New World in opposition to the Old World they had left behind. The history of settlement is broadly the history of westward movement, as new arrivals and restless pioneers sought to begin America again with their own exploration of the untamed continent. The Frontier has this physical reality, but it also has a psychological reality which has persisted long after the exhaustion of physical space to explore.

In 1893 Frederick Jackson Turner (1861–1932) published an essay entitled 'The Significance of the Frontier in American History'. He suggested that the Frontier had been responsible for producing a distinctive American spirit, relatively free from European influence and trained in the practical realities of democratic social organisation. The West, he argued, held the promise of freedom for all. It offered the means to live and possibilities for personal development. But at the time he was writing, Turner knew that the Frontier was effectively closed. Viewers of the television programme *Star Trek* with its adventures at the 'final frontier' will recognise how Americans have tried to meet this crisis by extending the Frontier into outer space.

F. Scott Fitzgerald relies upon our awareness of the Frontier hypothesis to generate an additional layer of meaning in his novel. Nick has gone East to seek material success, but has found life there unbearable, and has returned to the Midwest to write his book. The Midwest lies in the heart of the continent. It is distinct from the East Coast, but has its own West, unlike the West Coast, which has only the Pacific Ocean. Hollywood, in California on America's West Coast, may be seen as the place where America's dreams ended up, as real aspirations faded and celluloid fantasies took their place. The East Coast is the financial and business centre, with much stronger links to Europe. The Midwest connotes an authentic America whose values are old-fashioned yet conserve their integrity. These are values such as honesty and trust, and even a kind of innocence, which are embodied by Gatsby's father, Henry C. Gatz. Yet in Jay Gatsby's eyes his father is a failure.

If the East Coast beckoned to young Westerners such as Nick, promising success, then a still greater reversal of the Frontier's westward dynamic occurred with the First World War, which in 1917 took the descendants of New World settlers back to the Old World. It is significant that Jay Gatsby did very well in the war, and gained opportunities for social advancement that would not otherwise have arisen.

The novel is set on Long Island, and more specifically on the two Eggs, East being home to the Buchanans, while the less fashionable West is home to Gatsby and his neighbour, Nick Carraway. Thematically, the suggestion is that Gatsby's enormous capacity for hope places him ultimately in the idealistic tradition of the American Dream, and we are invited to believe that Nick belongs with him, in the West.

CHECK THE NET
For historical images of mansions on Long Island visit http://www. webscope.com/li/ mg.html

DESIRE AND THE SENSE OF PURPOSE

In addition to specifically American themes, F. Scott Fitzgerald addresses issues that concern all human beings, even though they are embedded in his depiction of a specifically American society. Gatsby's greatness, for Nick Carraway, resides in his capacity for hope and the strength of his desire.

Daisy is the immediate object of that desire, but Nick says that Gatsby's hunger for the possibilities life has to offer 'had gone beyond her, beyond everything' (Chapter 5, p. 92). He repeatedly stresses that to kiss this woman will not fulfil Gatsby: 'He knew that when he kissed this girl, and forever wed his unutterable visions to her perishable breath, his mind would never romp again like the mind of God' (Chapter 6, p. 107).

In short, his desire is a drive to transcend the world as it is, to move beyond it towards something better. That something cannot be defined or pinned down. But the act of striving for this unspecified goal creates an intensity which, Carraway suggests, bestows value on human experience.

It may have been the same passion that took the Dutch sailors to the New World, where, as the conclusion of the novel tells us, their sense of wonder found its reward, real yet not definable. America, in the process of its historical development, could never match the intensity of this initial experience of wonder.

F. Scott Fitzgerald contrasts the energy of Gatsby's desire with the apathy and cynicism of those around him. Daisy, still in her early twenties, complains that she has 'been everywhere and seen everything and done everything' (Chapter 1, p. 22). She cannot imagine that the future holds any promise for her, and the prospect of having to devise ways to while away the years ahead appals her. Her social set shares this purposelessness. They drift, restless but without direction. The only desire they know is that which is generated by advertisements, a desire for objects which they can readily afford. It is a trivial emotion and is soon extinguished or exhausted.

 CHECK THE NET http://www. questia.com/ PM.qst?action= openPageViewer& docId=27365140 offers a fascinating account of Hollywood's recurrent interest in Arthurian romance.

Gatsby, like a knight in Arthurian **romance**, has taken Daisy as his grail, the sacred object of his quest. Quest is one of the basic models for narrative structure. A hero sets out in search of some valued object and, although he or she meets with adventures and adversities along the way, remains single-minded in pursuit. In contrast with those who drift around him, Gatsby's life is directed and purposeful.

But it is a life that ends in tragedy. His energy is cancelled out by a murderer in a case of mistaken identity. We might conclude that such a life driven by hope is untenable in modern America, and decide that Gatsby was mistaken to pursue transcendence, especially as Daisy Buchanan was so obviously unworthy as an object of his devotion. But Nick's account shows a world of bored individuals, lacking any sense of purpose, and it emphasises the need for the kind of vision that might redeem this world from terminal apathy. Gatsby's desire sustains such a vision. Nick, despite his dismay at being thirty years old with thinning hair and diminishing prospects, finds purpose in his own life and devotes himself to the creative task of writing the story of Jay Gatsby.

VISION AND INSIGHT

F. Scott Fitzgerald explores vision in terms of physiological acts of perception, but also in terms of transcendent vision, the capacity of individuals and societies to envisage possibilities beyond the obvious and the given.

One of the most striking images in the novel is that of the eyes of Doctor T. J. Eckleburg, looming blindly over the 'valley of ashes' (Chapter 2, p. 26). This advertising hoarding is a realistic detail from the landscape of 1920s America, but it is also a haunting symbol in a novel that is crucially concerned with the possibilities and the limits of vision and with **point of view**.

The eyes, framed by spectacles, take on harrowing significance late in the book when George Wilson mistakes them for the eyes of God. He assumes that God is all-seeing, but these eyes are blind. F. Scott Fitzgerald seems to imply that this world is godless and there is no caring being who oversees our actions and ensures that justice is done.

In place of God's omniscience, F. Scott Fitzgerald presents a world of partial knowledge, of blinkered vision limited by point of view. Nick Carraway is presenting Gatsby's story as he saw it, but he knows there are other versions which might be told from other points of view. He declares that 'life is much more successfully looked at from a single window, after all' (Chapter 1, p. 10). It might be argued that singularity of vision is one of Gatsby's special qualities. But his vision is ultimately of a world beyond the material world that surrounds him, and in consequence he often seems to be blind to the actual nature of things.

The visitor to Gatsby's party who wears owl-eyed spectacles, as Nick sees and describes them, has the appearance of wisdom conventionally associated with the owl; his spectacles make him look scholarly. But the limits to his vision are very clear, and they are not just the consequence of drunkenness. He is impressed by the fact that Gatsby's library contains some real books but he is not interested in the contents of the books, nor is he interested in the single-minded vision that has driven Gatsby to use such props. Owl Eyes is content to be impressed by the man's stage management. He is one of the few mourners who attend Gatsby's funeral, but he does not really mourn. Instead he judges Gatsby to have been a 'poor son-of-a-bitch' (Chapter 9, p. 166). He can only see the mundane

CONTEXT

In ancient Greek mythology the owl was closely associated with Athena, goddess of wisdom. Athena's owl is today represented on the Greek one euro coin.

 CHECK THE NET

To see the image of an ancient coin depicting this symbolic owl visit http://www. davidicke.net/ symbolism/ancient/ owlcoin.html

reality, not the ideal which gave meaning to Gatsby's life. For him Gatsby was not tragic, but just a pathetic obsessive.

Following Gatsby's death, Nick tells us that he found the East Coast 'distorted beyond my eyes' power of correction' (Chapter 9, p. 167). Without Gatsby, all seems grotesque to him, like images painted by El Greco (1541–1614). It is possible that as readers we may wish to agree with the owl-eyed man, rather than accept Nick's elevated depiction of his hero. But we are left with the image at the end of the novel of the enchanted vision that met the eyes of the Dutch sailors arriving in the New World, and that is more difficult to dismiss. It returns us to Gatsby as an embodiment of the hope that such vision might somehow redeem the world from brutality and indifference.

CODES OF CONDUCT

At the start of his narration, Nick declares his belief in the need for codes of conduct to regulate human behaviour, and to control the unruly elements of our selves:

> And, after boasting this way of my tolerance, I come to the admission that it has a limit. Conduct may be founded on the hard rock or the wet marshes, but after a certain point I don't care what it's founded on. (Chapter 1, pp. 7–8)

He speaks of his wish for the world, after the turbulence of the war, 'to be in uniform and at a sort of moral attention forever' (Chapter 1, p. 8).

F. Scott Fitzgerald develops this theme in various ways as the novel progresses. The central issue is whether it is better to live a cautious and disciplined existence or to indulge in a passionate, unruly life. The former offers security, but it lacks the intensity of experience that comes with the latter. Nick's **ambivalence** towards Gatsby is really focused on this question of how best to live one's life. He deplores Gatsby's excesses, yet he cannot prevent himself admiring his reckless commitment.

This issue of whether it is better to lead a cautious or a passionate existence is raised in vivid terms in Joseph Conrad's *Heart of*

CONTEXT

El Greco (1541–1614) was born in Crete (hence his name, which means 'The Greek' in Spanish), but he lived and worked as a painter in Spain. An element of expressive distortion in his pictures makes them appear rather strange and striking. Some art historians have suggested that El Greco suffered from defective vision and painted in this mannered style as a consequence.

CHECK THE NET

Examples of El Greco's work can be found at http://www.ibiblio.org/wm/paint/auth/greco/

Darkness (1902), a novella that had a profound impact upon F. Scott Fitzgerald, who recognised its thematic seriousness and technical skill. *Heart of Darkness* has an unnamed narrator who relates a tale he heard from a sailor called Marlow. It concerns a European called Kurtz who lived a restrained life at home but when in Africa gave in to impulses that transgressed the limits of European codes of conduct and rules of decent behaviour.

Marlow is appalled by the downfall of Kurtz, yet there is an unsettling sense that Kurtz's impassioned and deplorable life was somehow more real than the morally constrained lives of those he left behind in Europe. Marlow, in his storytelling, makes Kurtz a larger than life figure in much the same way that Nick turns Gatsby into a kind of **mythic** presence in his story.

The theme of codes of conduct also leads us into *The Great Gatsby*'s investigation of the difficulties involved in being honest. Honesty is clearly a virtue, and it is seen to be lacking in many of the book's characters. Jordan cheats at golf, and Wolfshiem fixes the World Series. Sport is fundamentally dependent upon codes of conduct, but its codes are violated in these two cases. And what of Gatsby's **'old sport'**, which seems to invoke fair play, but is in fact a spurious affectation?

Nick takes pride in his own honesty. It is comforting to believe that we are reading an account written by a man we can trust. But what is the code that governs his sense of obligation to write this book? Is he really being honest about his reasons for admiring Jay Gatsby?

TECHNIQUES

THE NARRATOR

The most important literary technique utilised by F. Scott Fitzgerald in *The Great Gatsby* was recognised immediately by his editor. Maxwell Perkins, writing to the author in November 1924, remarked that he had adopted the most appropriate method of telling the story. He had decided to employ a narrator who was a participant in the story, but was more a spectator than an actor. This creates a complex **point of view**, which involves us, as readers,

CHECK THE BOOK

F. Scott Fitzgerald was also influenced by another of Joseph Conrad's works, the novel *Lord Jim* (1900).

in acts of interpretation that necessarily extend to making judgements about the narrator.

This technique was derived from Joseph Conrad, a writer F. Scott Fitzgerald admired, who had used a similar narrative technique in *Lord Jim* (1900) and in *Heart of Darkness* (1902) (see **Literary background**).

The success of the novel depends heavily upon F. Scott Fitzgerald's control of how the figure of Jay Gatsby is presented to us. He has to be filtered through Nick Carraway's narration at a suitable pace and with appropriate emphasis to sustain our interest without dispelling the necessary element of mystery. Expressing his reservations as well as his admiration at the outset, Nick himself becomes a figure whom we must interpret. So as we are piecing together the puzzle of Gatsby, we are inevitably adjusting our sense of the man who is telling Gatsby's story.

By making Nick a writer, F. Scott Fitzgerald combines an authorial capacity to comment and to pass judgement with the involved immediacy of the first-person voice. So we find him making carefully formulated and considered remarks such as:

> Instead of rambling, this party had preserved a dignified homogeneity, and assumed to itself the function of representing the staid nobility of the countryside – East Egg condescending to West Egg and carefully on guard against its spectroscopic gaiety. (Chapter 3, p. 46)

Then, a few pages after this wry commentary, we find Nick thoroughly caught up in events: 'I was enjoying myself now. I had taken two finger-bowls of champagne, and the scene had changed before my eyes into something significant, elemental, and profound' (Chapter 3, p. 48). He is still concerned to impress upon us the importance of events occurring in the narrative, but his seriousness is lightened by the image of his own light-headedness, and by the immediate sense of his own pleasure.

It is easy to imagine that if F. Scott Fitzgerald had been too precipitate in the narration, or had divulged too much (or too little)

QUESTION
Compare and contrast the districts of West Egg and East Egg.

at the wrong time, we would have a very different book, one in which Gatsby appeared a ridiculously comic or unequivocally sinister character. As it is, Gatsby, filtered through Carraway's narration, presents an intriguingly complex figure, and is able to carry the weight of associations from history and from myth that F. Scott Fitzgerald chooses to place upon him. Gatsby is simultaneously a man and an **archetype**, standing for America, and that is testimony to F. Scott Fitzgerald's considerable skill.

DIALOGUE AND THE SCENIC METHOD

Narrating the story from Nick Carraway's point of view, F. Scott Fitzgerald must have been acutely aware of certain dangers. For example, the voice of the narrator might have become monotonous, his manner of expression too insistent and self-conscious. F. Scott Fitzgerald avoids this pitfall by having Nick recreate dramatic exchanges in dialogue; as he writes his account, he mimics the idiosyncrasies of a range of voices. For example, Gatsby has the affectation of a nervous Anglophile, while Wolfshiem's voice is blatantly stylised as Jewish.

Similarly, if F. Scott Fitzgerald had written the account purely in terms of the working of Nick Carraway's mind, of his musings on the significance of what he has witnessed, then we would have a sluggish, even turgid, novel. The kind of self-analysis we meet in the opening paragraphs of the novel is fine for two pages, but if sustained for nearly two hundred it would surely deter many readers. So, F. Scott Fitzgerald has his narrator producing dramatic reconstructions in a series of linked scenes, rich in significant detail. The staging of his dramatic dialogues is organised through these set pieces.

F. Scott Fitzgerald adopted the scenic method of narrative construction which he admired in the work of the American novelists Henry James (1843–1916) and Edith Wharton (1862–1937). He presents a sequence of scenes, each self-contained, yet echoing others and containing elaborate cross-reference. This is easily understood if one considers the way in which the party in Chapter 2, in Myrtle's apartment, is paralleled by the party in the Plaza Hotel in Chapter 7. Larger parties are held at Gatsby's mansion, in Chapters 3 and 6. In this way, a structural symmetry is constructed. At the centre of the book, in Chapter 5, Nick and Daisy are reunited over tea at Nick's house.

QUESTION Consider ways in which F. Scott Fitzgerald frames the scenes in his book and how he handles transitions between them.

So Nick's recollection combines commentary, and analysis of the overall situation, with lively and varied dramatic scenes that feature skilfully crafted dialogue. The dialogue assists the unfolding of the story. It also serves to develop characterisation, granting insights into the nature and attitudes of the speakers. Invariably, Nick lets the speech stand without comment, leaving it to his readers to weigh the significance of what is said, and to draw their own conclusions.

CINEMATIC TECHNIQUES

F. Scott Fitzgerald's final novel, *The Last Tycoon* (1941), left unfinished at his death, is set in Hollywood, which he knew well through working there from 1937 as a scriptwriter. The advent of 'talkies' at the end of the 1920s drew numerous serious writers, including John Steinbeck (1902–68) and William Faulkner (1897–1962), to Hollywood, where their skill in scripting dialogue was in great demand. In *The Great Gatsby* he employs some techniques which might be indebted to the example of the cinema. The most evident is the cut, which he uses to make transitions from scene to scene, without obvious continuity. Chapter 4 furnishes good examples with the cut from Gatsby's car to a cellar where he has lunch with Wolfshiem (Chapter 4, p. 67), and the cut from that cellar to the Plaza Hotel where he is taking tea with Jordan (Chapter 4, p. 72).

The alternation between scenes in which small parties occur (at Myrtle's apartment and at the Plaza) and scenes in which the large parties are given by Gatsby might be read in terms of cinematic practice, moving from the close-up to the panoramic shot. This interpretation is particularly inviting as the parties at Gatsby's house are artificially lit like a stage or film set. Note the care with which F. Scott Fitzgerald handles lighting effects in his prose.

SYMBOLISM

Nick's narrative is rich in detail. But it is difficult when reading the novel to regard objects as objects pure and simple. F. Scott Fitzgerald has created an atmosphere of symbolism in which any object may resonate with additional significance. So, a shirt is not just a functional item of clothing, but is made to carry the weight of social class and of cosmopolitan sophistication. Similarly, a car is not just a vehicle for physical mobility, for moving from one place

CONTEXT

Arguably the finest and most dramatic fictional treatment of Hollywood was *The Day of the Locust* (1939) by Nathanael West (1903–40), a friend of F. Scott Fitzgerald.

TECHNIQUES

to another, it is also a symbol of social mobility, with large, flamboyant automobiles declaring the superiority of their drivers over the owners of more mundane ones. This kind of symbolic value is by no means an exclusively literary device: it is the essence of advertising, that modern practice of generating desires which features centrally in the novel.

F. Scott Fitzgerald's symbolism can assume a more narrowly literary aspect, however, as in the recurrent reference to roses, which have long served as a literary symbol for beauty and for femininity. *The Romance of the Rose*, a famous French poem of the Middle Ages, translated by Geoffrey Chaucer (c.1343–1400), indicates the pedigree of this literary convention. But in 1923, two years before the publication of *The Great Gatsby*, the American poet William Carlos Williams (1883–1963) published a poem, in a book called *Spring and All*, which began 'The rose is obsolete'. He meant that the symbol of the rose was no longer relevant to the way people live. Williams wanted to break away from traditional literary associations. He felt that by leaving behind inherited modes of expression, one could escape from conventional ways of understanding, and so establish more genuine contact with the world as it was experienced in the twentieth century. He saw the writer's task as a cleansing of language. The rose would again become simply a rose.

F. Scott Fitzgerald, on the other hand, was interested in the way that symbolism could produce a kind of magical transformation in which the physical world might, through an act of imagination, come to assume the quality of the ideal. So, towards the end of *The Great Gatsby*, when Gatsby's aspirations have been shattered by events, he looks at the world no longer filtered through symbolism and so robbed of its power of enchantment. Nick remarks, 'He must have looked up at an unfamiliar sky through frightening leaves and shivered as he found what a grotesque thing a rose is and how raw the sunlight was upon the scarcely created grass' (Chapter 8, p. 153).

F. Scott Fitzgerald often uses the familiar associations of symbols in ironic ways. An obvious example is the way he plays with the symbolic associations of the colour green. Green symbolises nature, fertility, growth and lushness in the organic world. It serves this

CHECK THE BOOK

Leo Marx's *The Machine in the Garden: Technology and the Pastoral Ideal in America* (OUP, 1964) is an informative study of literary responses to technology in light of the widely held view of the America West as an unspoilt garden. Marx includes a brief discussion of *The Great Gatsby* with its pointedly 'green' symbolism and its images of modern machinery.

SYMBOLISM continued

CHECK THE NET

For an index to *The Great Gatsby*, complete with explanatory notes and web links for more complex entries, see http://www.brtom.org/gg/ggind1.html

symbolic purpose without irony when F. Scott Fitzgerald makes reference to the fresh, green breast of the New World encountered once by Dutch sailors. That symbolic resonance of green is used ironically, however, when he writes of a green electric light at the end of the Buchanans' dock. The colour's symbolic association with envy or jealousy seems more relevant at that point, in that artificial environment, than green's evocation of the natural world.

INTRICATE PATTERNING

The composition of *The Great Gatsby* involves the development of complex structures of meaning, intricate patterns in which words and events foreshadow or echo others, often with considerable subtlety.

For example, colour words – notably green, white and gold – recur regularly, often applied to very different objects. The familiar associations of these colours are modified as the words appear in differing contexts. So white is applied to the 'palaces' of the wealthy (Chapter 1, p. 11), and to the 'ashen dust' that coats George Wilson's clothes (Chapter 2, p. 28). Daisy refers to her 'white girlhood' in the American South (Chapter 1, p. 24), which might appear to mean one thing in relation to her white dress (Chapter 1, p. 13), but quite another in the context of Tom's remarks on the supposed superiority of the white race (Chapter 1, p. 18).

Other threads are created through references to flowers, to clothing, to sight and vision, to accidents and carelessness, and so on. Despite the brevity of the novel, it achieves remarkable richness of meaning, and this patterning, with virtually every word being made carry some weight, is a major factor in its success.

Patterned language is more usually found in poetry, where the interplay of echoes and cross-references can generate a wealth of meaning. In novels that give priority to straightforward storytelling or to a documentary account of events, language plays a less complex role. F. Scott Fitzgerald did not always write with the intricacy he favours in *The Great Gatsby*. The prose of his short stories is far less rich and in his other novels he adopted more sober styles. Here intricate patterning serves his purpose of creating a diffuse glow of meaning and suggestion around the novel's events, rather than pinning them down once and for all, in line with a single interpretation. It also reveals that Nick Carraway has a poetic imagination beneath his rather prosaic surface.

CHARACTERISATION

The novel aims to present the way things appear from a particular **point of view**, rather than to offer objective description of the kind one might find in a novel which assumes that all points of view are pretty much the same. F. Scott Fitzgerald is interested in the differences that arise within different perspectives.

The point of view held by Nick Carraway is obviously the one that dominates in the novel, but we are not allowed to forget that other interpretations are possible. Tom Buchanan's view of Gatsby or Henry C. Gatz's view of his son is included in the account, for example, and shows how fundamentally different views of a single individual may be. Nick Carraway narrates the tale, and we derive a sense of what he is like from reading his words, but passing comments about him that he attributes to characters such as Daisy or Jordan may cast Nick in a very different light.

Characterisation is not therefore a straightforward business. Nick is engaged in a process of assessing character and of reading motivation. Occasionally he will offer, or imply, a judgement. But as with the case of Gatsby, his assessment might itself be difficult to interpret. He tells us that he is scornful of Gatsby, and in the next breath admits that he admired him intensely. We are given clues to read, such as the clothes characters wear, the things they own, the activities they engage in, their body language.

Then there is the dialogue which gives us a chance to look for tell-tale signs of character evident in the language used or the tone of delivery. Again, this is not straightforward. When Nick tells us that Daisy speaks 'with an expression of unthoughtful sadness' (Chapter 1, p. 18), it is by no means clear what response we should make. What exactly is 'unthoughtful sadness'? Is it good or bad? Reading Nick's own character is still more difficult. He cannot always be taken at face value; perhaps he should never be taken at face value.

CONTEXT

The narrator of Joseph Conrad's *Heart of Darkness* (1902), a novella that had a major impact upon the way F. Scott Fitzgerald wrote *The Great Gatsby*, says that for the unorthodox storyteller Marlow 'the meaning of an episode was not inside like a kernel, but outside, enveloping the tale which brought it out only as a glow brings out a haze'. Nick Carraway seems to share Marlow's understanding of how a tale should produce meaning through suggestiveness rather than statement of fact.

QUESTION
List the key characteristics associated through such verbal hints with each of the novel's main characters.

Characterisation is developed through nuance, through suggestion, and these insubstantial hints are anchored in certain key aspects of character that Nick provides for our assistance. So Daisy's voice is repeatedly referred to as holding the key clue to her character. Tom has a 'cruel body' (Chapter 1, p. 12), which reveals the kind of man he is. Jordan Baker is identified by her 'jaunty' bearing (Chapter 3, p. 58). And Gatsby has that smile, which carries so much significance in Nick's memory of him.

F. Scott Fitzgerald has made the complexity and difficulty of reading character a theme of the novel, as well as a technical concern.

PART FOUR

CRITICAL HISTORY

When F. Scott Fitzgerald died in 1940, his reputation as a writer was low. Obituaries tended to characterise him as a writer who had failed to fulfil his early promise. His decline into alcoholism was seen as somehow related to an incapacity to deal with mature subjects using mature literary craft. In fact, the writing which he regarded as his serious work was largely ignored, and the focus fell upon those entertaining, diverting but lightweight stories, which distinguished him as the chronicler of the Jazz Age.

It took little more than a decade following his death to establish F. Scott Fitzgerald as one of the major writers in the history of American literature. This change in the fortunes of his reputation was initially due largely to the efforts of his friend Edmund Wilson, who secured publication in 1941 for *The Last Tycoon*, the novel which F. Scott Fitzgerald left unfinished, and in 1945 for an important collection entitled *The Crack-Up*.

REACTIONS ON PUBLICATION

The Great Gatsby received more favourable reviews than any other of his books. Its critical reception was not matched by sales, but amongst enthusiastic readers, Gilbert Seldes, writing in the *Dial*, argued that F. Scott Fitzgerald had surpassed his contemporaries and had outstripped many of his predecessors in American writing. He received letters of praise from fellow writers including Gertrude Stein, Willa Cather and Edith Wharton, and from T. S. Eliot, who considered it the first significant advance in American fiction since Henry James.

In 1945 Lionel Trilling wrote an essay of appreciation in which he suggested that Gatsby could be taken as a figure who represented America itself. In 1954 this insight was developed by Marius Bewley in 'Scott Fitzgerald's Criticism of America'. The appearance of a series of biographies of F. Scott Fitzgerald has encouraged a strand of biographical criticism, identifying people and events that provided the writer with raw material for his fiction. There have

> **CONTEXT**
> Edmund Wilson (1895–1972), a friend from the college days of F. Scott Fitzgerald, was a prolific author, writing plays, poetry and travel books, although he remains best known for his influential works of social and literary criticism.

also been essays which have suggested literary influences on the composition of the novel, notably Joseph Conrad's fiction, the poetry of T. S. Eliot and John Keats, and a range of Christian and pagan myths. Other critics have focused upon formal aspects of the novel, with the role of the narrator being subjected to diverse and often provocative lines of argument. F. Scott Fitzgerald's language has also come under critical scrutiny.

RECENT APPROACHES

 CHECK THE BOOK

Scott Fitzgerald: The Promises of Life, edited by A. Robert Lee (St Martin's Press, 1989), brings together a variety of essays on F. Scott Fitzgerald and his work.

A list of critical books and essays on *The Great Gatsby* would now run to several hundred items, and yet the novel continues to stimulate analysis. More recent approaches have considered the role of women in the book, and the assumptions of the male voice which frames the depiction of relationships between the sexes. F. Scott Fitzgerald's treatment of race has also provided issues for debate. In both these cases it appears that the novelist is offering criticism of oppression in America – the violence committed by Tom against both Daisy and Myrtle is unequivocally brutal, while the racist views he offers in Chapter 2 are clearly treated with contempt by the author. But some critics have suggested that there is tacit endorsement beneath the ostensible condemnation, and that F. Scott Fitzgerald ultimately condones sexist and racist positions. The literary criticism fuels ongoing debate; it is testimony to the richness of the novel that it sustains such a range of discussion.

PART FIVE

BACKGROUND

F. SCOTT FITZGERALD

Francis Scott Key Fitzgerald was born in St Paul, Minnesota, on 24 September 1896. His father, Edward Fitzgerald, ran a furniture business, but that failed, and he moved to New York, where he became a salesman. In 1908 he lost that job, and the family returned to the Midwest.

F. Scott Fitzgerald entered the St Paul Academy in 1908, beginning a period of education that was largely financed by his mother's family. He started writing while at the school, finishing his first play in 1911. In that year he moved to Newman School, a Roman Catholic establishment in New Jersey, and in 1913 progressed to Princeton University.

At Christmas 1914 he met and fell in love with Ginevra King, a sixteen-year-old from a wealthy family in St Paul. She subsequently rejected him, because his family was not sufficiently rich. It is possible that F. Scott Fitzgerald is evoking this experience with a pun on the name King when Nick Carraway remarks: 'High in a white palace the king's daughter, the golden girl' (Chapter 7, p. 115).

In October 1917 F. Scott Fitzgerald received a commission as an infantry second lieutenant. In November he reported to Fort Leavenworth, Kansas, and began writing a novel entitled *The Romantic Egoist*.

In 1918 he reported to Camp Sheridan in Montgomery, Alabama, and in July he met there Zelda Sayre, who had been born there in 1900, and who subsequently became his wife. He was on Long Island, awaiting embarkation for Europe, when the end of the war was announced.

In February 1919 he was discharged from the army, and went to work for an advertising agency. He then returned to St Paul, and while living with his parents rewrote his novel, which was accepted

CONTEXT

Francis Scott Key Fitzgerald was named after Francis Scott Key (1779–1843), the writer of 'The Star-Spangled Banner' (adopted in 1931 as the US national anthem), and a distant relation of the Fitzgeralds.

 CHECK THE NET
http://www.pbs.org/kteh/amstorytellers/bios.html has a concise biography of Zelda Sayre.

by Maxwell Perkins at Scribner's, for publication as *This Side of Paradise*. It appeared in March 1920.

In April 1920 he married Zelda in New York, and began regularly to publish stories in magazines, making regular contributions to the *Saturday Evening Post*. In 1921 the couple paid their first visit to Europe, travelling in England, France and Italy. At the end of 1921 his second novel, *The Beautiful and Damned*, was serialised in *Metropolitan Magazine*, before appearing in book form in the following year.

In October 1921 their daughter Scottie was born. Between 1922 and 1924 the family rented a house in Great Neck, Long Island. This furnished experiences and encounters which later became raw material for *The Great Gatsby*.

In 1923 he published a play called *The Vegetable*. It was performed in Atlantic City, but was not successful. In 1924 the family returned to France, where F. Scott Fitzgerald began writing *The Great Gatsby*, which was completed, with revisions, in Rome at the beginning of 1925.

During the next few years, they travelled further in Europe, and ventured into North Africa. F. Scott Fitzgerald began to look for work in Hollywood, but in April 1930 Zelda had a mental breakdown in Paris and was admitted to a clinic in Switzerland. Her illness continued until the end of her life and necessitated extended periods in hospitals. During these spells of confinement she wrote a novel and painted.

F. Scott Fitzgerald's father died in 1931. His mother, Mollie, died five years later. Scottie pursued her education at school in Connecticut, and later at Vassar College. Meanwhile, F. Scott Fitzgerald built up considerable financial debts. He published *Tender is the Night* in 1934, and then reluctantly did freelance film work in Hollywood. At the same time he increasingly lapsed into alcoholism.

In October 1939 he began *The Last Tycoon*. On 21 December 1940 he died of a heart attack in Hollywood. He is buried in Rockville Union Cemetery in Maryland. Zelda died in a fire at the hospital in

CONTEXT

Numerous other American writers amongst Fitzgerald's contemporaries, including Ezra Pound (1885–1972), Gertrude Stein (1874–1946) and Ernest Hemingway (1899–1961), settled in Europe, perceiving it to be a place where literature and art were more highly valued than in America at that time.

which she was receiving treatment in 1948. She was buried with
F. Scott Fitzgerald.

HIS OTHER WORKS

F. Scott Fitzgerald wrote many short stories. They vary widely in
quality, from insubstantial pieces, dashed off to make money, to
enduring fictions such as 'The Diamond as Big as the Ritz' (1922).
The Great Gatsby is unquestionably his greatest achievement as a
novelist. The other novels appear flawed by comparison, but all are
accomplished works in differing ways.

This Side of Paradise (1920) was F. Scott Fitzgerald's first published
novel. It tells the story of Amory Blaine as he makes his way
through prep school to Princeton University, where he enters into
literary circles. He is sent to France during the First World War,
and then works in advertising. The novel drew heavily on F. Scott
Fitzgerald's own experiences, and was influenced by the British
writers H. G. Wells (1866–1946) and Compton Mackenzie
(1883–1972). The original title was *The Romantic Egotist*. The novel
was a popular success.

Critics have held *The Beautiful and Damned* (1922) to be his least
successful novel. It also derives much of its material from F. Scott
Fitzgerald's personal experiences, but he followed the literary
example of Theodore Dreiser to trace the harrowing physical and
spiritual decline of Anthony and Gloria Patch as they sink into
alcoholic dissolution.

Tender is the Night (1934) takes its title from John Keats's 'Ode to a
Nightingale', making explicit the affinity which F. Scott Fitzgerald
felt for the Romantic poet. The novel tells of the doomed
relationship of Dick and Nicole Diver. Dick served as an army
doctor during the First World War, and met Nicole while she
was a patient at a Swiss mental clinic. Nicole has further mental
breakdowns and eventually leaves her husband to marry Tommy
Barban. At the end of the novel Dick is an unsuccessful and
undistinguished doctor effectively buried alive in upstate New York.

The Last Tycoon was left unfinished at F. Scott Fitzgerald's death,
but was published, due to the efforts of Edmund Wilson, in 1941.

CONTEXT
F. Scott Fitzgerald's
first professional
story, 'Babes in
the Woods', was
published in
September 1919
in *The Smart Set*.

It is a portrait of Hollywood, its film industry and its decadent lifestyle. The protagonist, Monroe Stahr, is a memorable creation, despite the incomplete nature of the work.

'The Crack-Up' (1936), 'My Lost City' (published 1945) and 'Echoes of the Jazz Age' (1931) are remarkable essays, which should be consulted by any student of F. Scott Fitzgerald's work.

HISTORICAL BACKGROUND

THE JAZZ AGE AND THE LOST GENERATION

 CHECK THE NET
An excellent overview of the Jazz Age can be found at http://faculty. pittstate.edu/ ~knichols/jazzage. html

The decade following the First World War in America has become popularly known as the Jazz Age. Jazz music set exalted standards in terms of musicianship during the 1920s, especially in the soloing of trumpeter Louis Armstrong (1901–71) and the compositions of Duke Ellington (1899–1974), but affluent, young white Jazz Age listeners tended to favour a diluted form of the music, danceable, exuberant and carefree.

The 1920s were also known at the time as the Golden Twenties or the Roaring Twenties. F. Scott Fitzgerald played a major role in characterising these years as a period of pleasure seeking, and of reckless exuberance. Many of his short stories provide an entertaining picture of youthful hedonism and especially the antics of those liberated young women known as 'flappers', affronting conventional values with their short skirts, short hair and make-up. But in his more substantial fiction a far more gloomy and at times sinister version of the age emerges.

Gertrude Stein, an American writer living in Paris, referred to the Lost Generation of the post-First World War world. The novel usually cited as capturing the essence of this Lost Generation is *The Sun Also Rises* (1926), by F. Scott Fitzgerald's close friend, Ernest Hemingway. Hemingway depicts a group of expatriate Americans, wandering aimlessly through Europe, sensing that they are powerless and that life is pointless in the aftermath of the Great War. But the feeling of loss and emptiness had already been identified by F. Scott Fitzgerald when, at the end of his first novel,

This Side of Paradise (1920), he wrote of a new generation 'grown up to find all Gods dead, all wars fought, all faiths in man shaken'.

The Great Gatsby may also be seen to encapsulate this perception of life without purpose, of restlessness, dissatisfaction and drifting. It is this general ennui that makes Jay Gatsby's capacity for hope appear such a rare quality. The novel was published in the middle of the decade, and reveals a mindless quest for pleasure and a loss of direction in life to be two sides of the same coin. As F. Scott Fitzgerald shows so memorably, the indulgence of the 1920s in all forms of excess was never far from a collapse into desperation.

ADVERTISING AND THE MASS MARKET

The population of America more or less doubled in the half-century before *The Great Gatsby* was published. The nation had to face the problem of how to meet the basic requirements of this growing population, and one solution came in the development of mass-production techniques in factories. In 1913, Henry Ford first used an assembly line to produce his Model T automobile, but the technique was already well established in the production of other goods for the mass market.

F. Scott Fitzgerald's novel was written against the background of this explosive growth in commodities available for purchase, most of which were standardised products. Standardisation seemed appropriate to a modern democracy, where all citizens might have the right to buy items which were available to all. Companies and large stores based in big cities produced catalogues that enabled Americans living in remote areas to make mail-order purchases.

The early years of the century saw a corresponding change in advertising. Products were given brand names, often promoted as a sign of reliability. In 1903 an academic psychologist named William Dill Scott published *The Theory and Practice of Advertising*, following it up in 1908 with *The Psychology of Advertising*. Such studies signalled a fundamental change of approach. Advertising had for a long time been intended to inform potential buyers what was available for purchase. But new advertising techniques sought to create the desire for commodities, to shape the taste of the nation rather than merely to reflect it.

CHECK THE NET
Salient points concerning the Lost Generation are to be found at http://ok. essortment.com/ whatlostgenera_ nkj.htm

CHECK THE BOOK
An excellent illustrated account of the development of advertising techniques and strategies in America during this period is Susan Strasser's book *Satisfaction Guaranteed: The Making of the American Mass Market* (Pantheon, 1989).

Packaging became much more important, designed to entice potential buyers, and salesmen were trained in new marketing techniques, new means to persuasion. In 1927 the American writer Sinclair Lewis (1885–1951) published a novel entitled *Elmer Gantry*, whose hero combines the techniques of persuasion of the salesman and of the evangelist with masterly cynicism.

F. Scott Fitzgerald created Jay Gatsby at a time when the American workplace was increasingly ruled by doctrines of scientific management, by time and motion studies which aimed to gain maximum efficiency from workers. Henry Ford actually employed a team to monitor the private lives of his workers, to ensure that energies were not being squandered during the hours of leisure.

Gatsby is a figure whose sense of time is not reflected on any clock face; he is a romantic figure who transcends the standardised, regulated world that was a reality for many Americans at the time. But he surely belongs to the brave new world of American advertising, for his act of self-creation can be seen as new packaging, the shift from Gatz to Gatsby as a change of brand name, while the mansion and the parties are strategies of marketing. He rises above the marketplace of his time in the sense that he is creating a unique product, intended not for mass consumption, but for Daisy Fay.

CONSPICUOUS CONSUMPTION

The term 'conspicuous consumption' was coined by a social scientist named Thorstein Veblen (1857–1929). Born in the American Midwest in 1857, he published a book in 1899 entitled *The Theory of the Leisure Class*. It was a response to the rise to power in America of extremely rich businessmen, who displayed their wealth in ostentatious houses and extravagant behaviour. This display Thorstein Veblen called 'conspicuous consumption', and he was critical of it on the grounds that it was invariably wasteful, and because, in his view, it implied increasing poverty amongst the lower classes in society.

The Great Gatsby presents a graphic illustration of how conspicuous consumption might become a measure of social status. Tom Buchanan, who is certainly a member of the leisure class, so wealthy that he does not need to work, has a team of polo ponies which he takes with him on his travels. They provide him with entertainment, but they also announce his status to others. Jay Gatsby has his mansion, he stages lavish parties and he is proud of a new hydroplane. The flamboyance of his lifestyle is seemingly remote from the drab world inhabited by George Wilson. The worlds collide in the accident that kills Myrtle, and it is yet another example of conspicuous consumption, Gatsby's expensive car, that leads Wilson to his victim.

PROHIBITION AND ORGANISED CRIME

At the time *The Great Gatsby* appeared, the production and sale of alcoholic drinks were prohibited in America. This Prohibition commenced on 16 January 1920, following the passing of the Volstead Act a year earlier. Prohibition, championed by the Anti-Saloon League, was intended to raise the nation's moral standards, but to a large extent it had the opposite effect. In practice it was difficult to enforce and it was not difficult for drinkers to find alcohol, as F. Scott Fitzgerald's novel makes very clear. In 1925 there were apparently one hundred thousand speakeasies, as unlawful drinking dens were called, in New York alone. Bootlegging, the illicit production and provision of alcohol, became big business, making fortunes for criminals such as the gangster Al Capone. This appears to be the principal source of Gatsby's wealth, the core of corruption within his lifestyle.

The illegal economy was organised by powerful gangs of criminals, who engaged in other unlawful activities such as gambling and protection rackets. In reality, figures such as Capone and 'Legs' Diamond became legends. They provided models for the gangster movies of the 1930s such as *Little Caesar* (1930), *Public Enemy* (1931) and *Scarface* (1932). Celebrity did not conceal the fact that these were ruthless and extremely dangerous men.

In *The Great Gatsby* the criminal underworld is represented by Meyer Wolfshiem, based on the real-life gambler Arnold Rothstein. His Jewishness is significant as F. Scott Fitzgerald seems to be indicating that while legitimate power in America is held exclusively by Anglo-Saxon men, the 'Nordics' (Chapter 1, p. 18) with whom Tom Buchanan identifies civilisation, the only route to prosperity open to members of other racial and cultural groups is

> **CONTEXT**
>
> The prominence of southern Europeans and Jewish Americans amongst the leaders of organised crime in America during the 1920s may perhaps be taken as a measure of their restricted access to legally sanctioned positions of power, wealth and influence. Such renowned figures as Al Capone (1899–1947), Lucky Luciano (1897–1962) and Meyer Lansky (1902–83) took an alternative route and placed themselves outside the law. In *The Great Gatsby* the Jewish gangster Meyer Wolfshiem is based on another historical figure, the corrupt gambler Arnold Rothstein (1882–1928).

CHECK THE BOOK

Michael Woodiwiss's *Organized Crime, United States of America: Changing Perceptions from Prohibition to the Present Day* (British Association for American Studies Pamphlet 19, 1990) is a handy overview of the topic.

CONTEXT

Amusement parks were the precursors of modern theme parks and usually featured all the attractions of the fun fair. They were extremely popular in America between the beginning of the twentieth century and the end of the 1920s, when a major downturn in the economy led to their decline. Steeplechase Park and Luna Park, located at Coney Island, New York, were still attracting vast crowds at the time F. Scott Fitzgerald wrote *The Great Gatsby*.

crime. A critical reading might argue that F. Scott Fitzgerald is endorsing racial stereotypes in these depictions, and is actually fuelling distrust. Still, there is historical evidence that Prohibition actually provided a means to advancement for ambitious Americans who were excluded from lawful and institutional channels, and bootlegging certainly became an extremely lucrative national industry. Prohibition was repealed in 1933.

MASS CULTURE

In the 1920 census America was shown, for the first time, to be an urban nation, with more people living in cities than in the countryside. It is true that some of the places classified as cities were actually moderate-sized towns, but nonetheless the trend towards an urban America was unmistakable. The growth of the population due to immigration from southern and eastern Europe, and the continuing flow of black Americans from the South, where their families had formerly been held in slavery, caused rapid and highly visible expansion of urban areas. The anonymity fostered by city living, where a citizen is just one amongst many, coupled with the increasing standardisation of production techniques, contributed to the sense that America had entered a new phase in its history, in which culture belonged to the masses.

Millionaires such as John Pierpont Morgan (1837–1913) and John D. Rockefeller (1839–1937) – both of whom F. Scott Fitzgerald mentions in the novel – might build unique art collections in the manner of Old World aristocrats, but Americans generally flocked to the moving pictures of the flourishing film industry. They read mass-circulation newspapers and magazines (such as *Town Tattle*, which Myrtle Wilson reads) that imposed unprecedented uniformity on the information reaching Americans across the continent. They spent their money to watch sporting spectacles, or indulged in the pleasures of the gaudy new amusement parks, such as Coney Island.

In response to the consolidation of America's urban masses, John Dos Passos (1896–1970) wrote *Manhattan Transfer* (1925), a novel of mass society, without a hero, while F. Scott Fitzgerald made a different decision and created the figure known as 'The Great Gatsby'.

PHOTOGRAPHS

Photographs of a crude kind were produced as far back as the 1820s.
Their evolution was vastly accelerated when, at the end of the 1870s,
a young American bank clerk called George Eastman (1854–1932)
became interested in photography. Within a short while he made a
series of crucial innovations that revolutionised the practice, making
it more readily available to all who could afford the basics and
extending its potential as a means for art. Eastman was not the only
significant figure active in photography at this time but he was a
well-known one and made a real difference.

In 1888 he patented a new camera, relatively small, conveniently
box-shaped and using strips of film rather than cumbersome plates.
He coined the trademark Kodak to launch this vastly improved
photographic system. A craze for taking photographs soon
followed, especially after Eastman introduced the Brownie camera
in 1900. By the 1920s, when important advances were being made in
motion pictures, still photography was widespread as a hobby and it
played a key part in cultivating contemporary America's fascination
with the glamorous image, encountered in newspapers, magazines
and advertisements.

Photography provides a recurrent motif in *The Great Gatsby*.
The thematic significance of the photograph is that it appears to
freeze time, and frames an experience which is preserved for later
contemplation. Gatsby has a photograph of Cody upon his wall,
and his father carries a picture of Gatsby's mansion.

But such photographs can be seen as **metaphors** for the vision
that makes Gatsby great. He has dedicated his life to pursuit of
a moment which was actually frozen in his past, the moment
he fell in love with Daisy. But his is not a passive contemplation;
rather it is dynamic, as if Gatsby wishes to break through the
frame and so recapture the instant caught by the camera of his
imagination.

In contrast to Gatsby's dynamism, the photographer McKee is a
failed artist. His photographs belong to a world of purposeless
despair, and have tell-tale names such as 'Loneliness' and 'Brooklyn

 CHECK THE NET
The history of
Coney Island is
recounted at
**http://naid.sppsr.
ucla.edu/
coneyisland/**

Bridge'. The bridge was a symbol of American modernity realised in the language of engineering, but it was also the site of numerous suicides. In fiction, a character named Bud Korpening leaps from the bridge to his death in *Manhattan Transfer* by John Dos Passos, also published in 1925.

LITERARY BACKGROUND

CHECK THE BOOK

Joseph Conrad's novella *Heart of Darkness* (1902) and his novel *Lord Jim* (1900) in particular had a great influence upon F. Scott Fitzgerald.

Contemporary commentators and more recent critics have remarked upon the striking difference between F. Scott Fitzgerald's first two novels and *The Great Gatsby*. It has been generally accepted that the advance is basically one of technical resourcefulness. F. Scott Fitzgerald had become a far more skilful and controlled writer. It should not diminish our sense of his achievement to recognise his debt to the novelist Joseph Conrad (1857–1924), a debt that F. Scott Fitzgerald himself readily acknowledged. Joseph Conrad was born in Poland, but lived and worked in England, and he aimed in his writing to raise the English novel to the level of seriousness attained by practitioners in France, such as Gustave Flaubert (1821–80). Joseph Conrad regarded the novel as a very serious form of artistic endeavour, one that could respond appropriately to the complex reality of the modern world. His best-known expression of the seriousness of the novelist's art is to be found in a preface written in 1897 for his novella *The Nigger of the 'Narcissus'*. F. Scott Fitzgerald read that preface while writing *The Great Gatsby*, and drew from it support for his own aspirations.

Joseph Conrad's preface opens with the assertion that any literary work that claims the status of art should carry its justification in every line; there should be no word or phrase that does not contribute to the overall meaning of the work. This neatly summarises the literary faith that informs F. Scott Fitzgerald's third novel, and makes it such a dramatic advance on *This Side of Paradise* and *The Beautiful and Damned*.

F. Scott Fitzgerald followed Joseph Conrad's example in producing a novel carefully composed through the intricate patterning of language and of narrative events. He also adopted the model used

by Joseph Conrad in *Lord Jim* (1900) and, with still more
sophistication, in *Heart of Darkness* (1902), of the narrator who is
also a participant in the story, and whose point of view demands the
reader's attention and interpretation. This important technical issue
of narrative point of view was also explored by Joseph Conrad's
English friend and collaborator Ford Madox Ford (1873–1939),
notably in *The Good Soldier* (1915), and by the expatriate American
novelist Henry James (1843–1916). Henry James also developed the
scenic method, constructing narrative through a series of
interlocking set pieces. F. Scott Fitzgerald was aware of the
technique in Henry James's novels and in the work of Edith
Wharton (1862–1937), notably *Ethan Frome* (1911).

F. Scott Fitzgerald was writing during the period of intensive
experimentation with literary forms and techniques, classified
as Modernism. He admired the work of radical innovators such
as Gertrude Stein (1874–1946) and James Joyce (1882–1941),
but his own approach to writing in *The Great Gatsby* is closer
to the example of Henry James, Ford Madox Ford and
Joseph Conrad.

A number of critics have suggested that the novel is indebted to
T. S. Eliot's Modernist poem *The Waste Land* (1922), but the debt
seems to be more in terms of the portrayal of the 'valley of ashes'
(Chapter 2, p. 26) as a sterile, spiritually desolate landscape, than
of a technical or formal nature. F. Scott Fitzgerald did send a
copy of the novel to T. S. Eliot, inscribed to the 'Greatest of
Living Poets'.

A case might be made for drawing a parallel between Nick
Carraway and the character J. Alfred Prufrock in T. S. Eliot's
poem 'The Love Song of J. Alfred Prufrock' (1917). They share
a combination of reticence and desire that leaves them
painfully inactive, wanting to make a move but unable to do
so. Nick, like Prufrock, panics at the prospect of growing old,
and they share the sense that they were not meant to be central
players upon life's stage. Nick, however, has found in Gatsby a
surrogate self.

> **CONTEXT**
>
> F. Scott Fitzgerald
> sent a copy of *The
> Great Gatsby* to
> Edith Wharton,
> who praised it
> as a masterly
> achievement.

T. S. Eliot (1888–1965), like Henry James, was an American who chose to live in England. Henry James actually made the comparison of Old and New World cultures the central theme of his work, the 'international theme' as he called it. F. Scott Fitzgerald follows that lead in *The Great Gatsby*, measuring American values against those European models which feature so prominently. He was, after all, a self-consciously American writer, aware of a distinctive American literary tradition to which he was adding.

The Great Gatsby can be read as a **romance**, and Nathaniel Hawthorne provided a valuable definition of that kind of writing (see **Reading** *The Great Gatsby*). Nathaniel Hawthorne felt that 'romance' was the appropriate mode for American authors, who did not, in the mid nineteenth century, have the complex structure of social relationships which sustained European novels, such as those of Sir Walter Scott or Jane Austen. American society in the 1920s had developed sufficiently to provide F. Scott Fitzgerald with ample material, but he nonetheless felt that romance preserved something quintessentially American.

CONTEXT

In a letter written to his aunt and uncle, dated 28 December 1920, F. Scott Fitzgerald described Mencken as 'my current idol'.

He combines romance with some biting social **satire**, and in this he had a model in H. L. Mencken (1880–1956), a caustic commentator on American life, whom F. Scott Fitzgerald greatly admired. He was upset when H. L. Mencken, reviewing *The Great Gatsby*, found it little more than 'a glorified anecdote'.

F. Scott Fitzgerald's close friend Ernest Hemingway (1899–1961) was an important stylist and a trenchant commentator upon contemporary American life; even when his novels are set in Europe and seem to pass no judgements upon the characters and events within them, they imply a great deal. Ernest Hemingway's *The Sun Also Rises* (1926) is the key novel depicting the Lost Generation, post-war Americans lingering in the Old World, drifting through life without purpose or beliefs.

Another strand of American writing that must be mentioned here is the rags-to-riches story, exemplified by Horatio Alger (1832–99). In a series of popular novels written specifically for boys, Horatio

Alger expounded the faith that the cultivation of a good moral character could enable young Americans to rise from poverty to wealth. F. Scott Fitzgerald's James Gatz follows the same path, but succeeds only through criminal means. *The Great Gatsby* challenges the moral naivety of the Horatio Alger books.

www. CHECK THE NET
http://www.online-literature.com/fitzgerald/greatgatsby/ has a thought-provoking section devoted to comments and reviews of *The Great Gatsby* by general readers.

World events	F. Scott Fitzgerald's life	Literary events
1918 First World War ends	**1918** Stationed at Camp Sheridan in Montgomery, Alabama	
1919 Baseball World Series is fixed	**1919** Discharged from the army and starts working for an advertising agency	
1920 Prohibition of alcohol commences in the USA (and continues until 1933) US women are given the right to vote	**1920** Marries Zelda Sayre Publication of F. Scott Fitzgerald's first novel *This Side of Paradise* Publication of the short-story collection *Flappers and Philosophers*	**1920** Publication of the novel *The Age of Innocence* by Edith Wharton
1921 Silent movie *The Kid*, starring Charlie Chaplin	**1921** Visits Europe	
	1922 Publication of the novel *The Beautiful and Damned* Publication of the short-story collection *Tales of the Jazz Age*	**1922** Publication of the poem *The Waste Land* by T. S. Eliot
	1923 Performance of the play *The Vegetable* is not a success Starts work on **The Great Gatsby**	**1923** Publication of the novel *The Rover* by Joseph Conrad

World events	F. Scott Fitzgerald's life	Literary events
	1924 Moves to the French Riviera	**1924** Publication of the novel *Some Do Not* by Ford Madox Ford
	1925 Publication of **The Great Gatsby**	**1925** Publication of the novel *An American Tragedy* by Theodore Dreiser
		Publication of the novel *Manhattan Transfer* by John Dos Passos
1926 Death of the matinée idol Rudolph Valentino	**1926** Publication of the short-story collection *All the Sad Young Men*	**1926** Publication of the novel *The Sun Also Rises* by Ernest Hemingway
1927 Charles Lindbergh makes the first solo transatlantic flight		**1927** Publication of the novel *Elmer Gantry* by Sinclair Lewis
1929 The Wall Street Crash – the collapse of the New York stock exchange heralds world economic depression		**1929** Publication of the novel *A Farewell to Arms* by Ernest Hemingway
1930 Work starts on the Empire State Building in New York		
Little Caesar, a gangster movie, appears		

OTHER WORKS BY F. SCOTT FITZGERALD

This Side of Paradise (1920)

Flappers and Philosophers (1920)

The Beautiful and Damned (1922)

Tales of the Jazz Age (1922)

All the Sad Young Men (1926)

Tender is the Night (1934)

Taps at Reveille (1935)

The Last Tycoon (1941)

The Crack-Up (1945)

The novels and collected short stories of F. Scott Fitzgerald are available in paperback editions published by Penguin Books.

The Letters of F. Scott Fitzgerald, edited by Andrew Turnbull, Penguin, 1968

BIOGRAPHIES

Matthew J. Bruccoli, *Some Sort of Epic Grandeur: The Life of F. Scott Fitzgerald*, Harcourt Brace Jovanovich, 1981; paperback, Cardinal Books, 1991
> A highly readable and authoritatively informative biography, which conveys a vivid sense of F. Scott Fitzgerald and his time. Contains photographs

André le Vot, *F. Scott Fitzgerald: A Biography*, translated by William Byron, Penguin, 1985
> A less direct account of the author's life, which includes some useful critical insights into the work

GENERAL READING

Marcus Cunliffe, *The Literature of the United States*, fourth edition, Penguin, 1986
  A reliable guide to the history of American literature, including F. Scott Fitzgerald's place within it

Mark Holloway, *Heavens on Earth: Utopian Communities in America, 1680–1880*, Dover Publications, 1966
  A fascinating account of various American attempts to realise an ideal society

Maldwyn A. Jones, *American Immigration*, University of Chicago Press, 1992
  Lively, illustrated history of the process of immigration that created modern America

D. H. Lawrence, *Studies in Classic American Literature*, Penguin, 1977; first published 1923
  Published before *The Great Gatsby* and concerned with nineteenth-century literature, but it offers very helpful insights into the nature of American idealism and American materialism

R. W. B. Lewis, *The American Adam: Innocence, Tragedy, and Tradition in the Nineteenth Century*, University of Chicago Press, 1955
  This is a classic study of the recurrence of the biblical figure of Adam as a thematic touchstone in nineteenth-century American literature. Lewis shows that Gatsby, F. Scott Fitzgerald's deeply ironic Adam, had numerous precursors in American writing

Michael McKeon, ed., *Theory of the Novel: A Historical Approach*, Johns Hopkins University Press, 2000

Leo Marx, *The Machine in the Garden: Technology and the Pastoral Ideal in America*, Oxford University Press, 1964
  An informative study of literary responses to technology in light of the widely held view of the America West as an unspoilt garden. Marx includes a brief discussion of *The Great Gatsby*

Henry Nash Smith, *Virgin Land: The American West as Symbol and Myth*, Harvard University Press, 1971
  Smith tells how the West acquired profound significance within America's perception of itself

Susan Strasser, *Satisfaction Guaranteed: The Making of the American Mass Market*, Pantheon, 1989
  An entertaining and informative history of the emergence of consumerism in America, which contains much that is pertinent to *The Great Gatsby*

GENERAL READING continued

Tony Tanner, *The Reign of Wonder*, Cambridge University Press, 1965
 A study of 'wonder' as a key quality addressed in American literature throughout its history

Michael Woodiwiss, *Organized Crime, United States of America: Changing Perceptions from Prohibition to the Present Day*, British Association for American Studies Pamphlet 19, 1990
 A brief, convenient summary of the topic

CRITICAL STUDIES

Ronald Berman, *The Great Gatsby and Modern Times*, University of Illinois Press, 1994
 Places the novel in the context of its time and place

Harold Bloom, ed., *F. Scott Fitzgerald's The Great Gatsby*, Modern Critical Interpretations, Chelsea House, 1986
 A series of provocative and stimulating essays

Jeffrey Louis Decker, 'Gatsby's Pristine Dream: The Diminishment of the Self-Made Man in the Tribal Twenties', *Novel*, Fall 1994, pp. 52–71
 An essay which engages critically with issues of race raised by the novel

Scott Donaldson, ed., *Critical Essays on F. Scott Fitzgerald's The Great Gatsby*, G. K. Hall, 1984
 An invaluable collection of key documents in the history of criticism of *The Great Gatsby*

Hugh Kenner, *A Homemade World: The American Modernist Writers*, Marion Boyars, 1977
 A stimulating discussion by a major literary critic

A. Robert Lee, ed., *Scott Fitzgerald: The Promises of Life*, St Martin's Press, 1989
 Varied selection of new essays on F. Scott Fitzgerald and his work

Robert E. Long, *The Achieving of The Great Gatsby: F. Scott Fitzgerald, 1920–25*, Bucknell University Press, 1979
 Primarily a study of literary influences, especially that of Joseph Conrad

ambivalence the coexistence in one person of two different attitudes to the same object or wish

anti-hero a character whose interest resides in the inability to perform deeds of bravery, or courage, or generosity. The unheroic protagonist has been widely explored in twentieth-century literature

archetype a typical or representative figure of a particularly imposing kind. The term may also refer to a typical or representative theme, image or plot

documentary realism writing that seeks to reconstruct actual events with factual accuracy, rather than creating fictional events or portraying actual events coloured by imagination or invention

irony to say one thing while meaning another, for example to use words of praise as a criticism or condemnation

metaphor describing one thing as being another. This goes further than a simile by merging two objects, for example 'the soldier was a lion in battle'

mythic belonging to myth, that is to stories that lay claim to truth beyond the influence of historical circumstances

naturalism a post-Darwinian mode of realism, in which human beings are seen as victims of impersonal forces such as heredity, disease or historical change, and their aspirations are seen as meaningless

oxymoron a figure of speech which combines two apparently contradictory terms, for example 'a wise fool'

paradox an apparently self-contradictory statement, or one that seems in conflict with logic, behind which lies a meaning or truth

point of view the way in which a narrator positions herself or himself in order to approach the materials forming a narrative and deliver them to readers. Examining the point of view helps us to understand how events are filtered through the narrator

romance a narrative that departs from the dictates of reality as it is known to common sense in order to evoke a magical world (see the description taken from Nathaniel Hawthorne in **Reading** *The Great Gatsby*)

satire literature which exposes or holds up to ridicule the follies and foibles of human beings

simile a kind of **metaphorical** writing in which one thing is said to be like another thing. Similes always compare two things and contain the words 'like' or 'as'. For example: 'the soldier was like a lion in battle'

Utopia a depiction of an imagined ideal world, or of a world that is perceived to be better than the one we know

Readers requiring further information on these, and other, terms are directed to Martin Gray's *A Dictionary of Literary Terms* (second edition), York Press, 1992, which has been used in compiling this glossary.

AUTHOR OF THESE NOTES

Julian Cowley holds a BA Hons from University College London, an MA from the Institute of United States Studies and a PhD from King's College London. For fifteen years he was a university lecturer on English and American Literature. He is now a freelance writer on literature and music.

General editor

Martin Gray, former Head of the Department of English Studies at the University of Stirling, and of Literary Studies at the University of Luton

Maya Angelou
I Know Why the Caged Bird Sings

Jane Austen
Pride and Prejudice

Alan Ayckbourn
Absent Friends

Elizabeth Barrett Browning
Selected Poems

Robert Bolt
A Man for All Seasons

Harold Brighouse
Hobson's Choice

Charlotte Brontë
Jane Eyre

Emily Brontë
Wuthering Heights

Shelagh Delaney
A Taste of Honey

Charles Dickens
David Copperfield
Great Expectations
Hard Times
Oliver Twist

Roddy Doyle
Paddy Clarke Ha Ha Ha

George Eliot
Silas Marner
The Mill on the Floss

Anne Frank
The Diary of a Young Girl

William Golding
Lord of the Flies

Oliver Goldsmith
She Stoops to Conquer

Willis Hall
The Long and the Short and the Tall

Thomas Hardy
Far from the Madding Crowd
The Mayor of Casterbridge
Tess of the d'Urbervilles
The Withered Arm and other Wessex Tales

L.P. Hartley
The Go-Between

Seamus Heaney
Selected Poems

Susan Hill
I'm the King of the Castle

Barry Hines
A Kestrel for a Knave

Louise Lawrence
Children of the Dust

Harper Lee
To Kill a Mockingbird

Laurie Lee
Cider with Rosie

Arthur Miller
The Crucible
A View from the Bridge

Robert O'Brien
Z for Zachariah

Frank O'Connor
My Oedipus Complex and Other Stories

George Orwell
Animal Farm

J.B. Priestley
An Inspector Calls
When We Are Married

Willy Russell
Educating Rita
Our Day Out

J.D. Salinger
The Catcher in the Rye

William Shakespeare
Henry IV Part I
Henry V
Julius Caesar
Macbeth
The Merchant of Venice
A Midsummer Night's Dream
Much Ado About Nothing
Romeo and Juliet
The Tempest
Twelfth Night

George Bernard Shaw
Pygmalion

Mary Shelley
Frankenstein

R.C. Sherriff
Journey's End

Rukshana Smith
Salt on the snow

John Steinbeck
Of Mice and Men

Robert Louis Stevenson
Dr Jekyll and Mr Hyde

Jonathan Swift
Gulliver's Travels

Robert Swindells
Daz 4 Zoe

Mildred D. Taylor
Roll of Thunder, Hear My Cry

Mark Twain
Huckleberry Finn

James Watson
Talking in Whispers

Edith Wharton
Ethan Frome

William Wordsworth
Selected Poems

A Choice of Poets

Mystery Stories of the Nineteenth Century including The Signalman

Nineteenth Century Short Stories

Poetry of the First World War

Six Women Poets

For the AQA Anthology:

Duffy and Armitage & Pre-1914 Poetry

Heaney and Clarke & Pre-1914 Poetry

Poems from Different Cultures

Margaret Atwood
Cat's Eye
The Handmaid's Tale

Jane Austen
Emma
Mansfield Park
Persuasion
Pride and Prejudice
Sense and Sensibility

Alan Bennett
Talking Heads

William Blake
Songs of Innocence and of Experience

Charlotte Brontë
Jane Eyre
Villette

Emily Brontë
Wuthering Heights

Angela Carter
Nights at the Circus

Geoffrey Chaucer
The Franklin's Prologue and Tale
The Merchant's Prologue and Tale
The Miller's Prologue and Tale
The Prologue to the Canterbury Tales
The Wife of Bath's Prologue and Tale

Samuel Coleridge
Selected Poems

Joseph Conrad
Heart of Darkness

Daniel Defoe
Moll Flanders

Charles Dickens
Bleak House
Great Expectations
Hard Times

Emily Dickinson
Selected Poems

John Donne
Selected Poems

Carol Ann Duffy
Selected Poems

George Eliot
Middlemarch
The Mill on the Floss

T.S. Eliot
Selected Poems
The Waste Land

F. Scott Fitzgerald
The Great Gatsby

E.M. Forster
A Passage to India

Brian Friel
Translations

Thomas Hardy
Jude the Obscure
The Mayor of Casterbridge
The Return of the Native
Selected Poems
Tess of the d'Urbervilles

Seamus Heaney
Selected Poems from 'Opened Ground'

Nathaniel Hawthorne
The Scarlet Letter

Homer
The Iliad
The Odyssey

Aldous Huxley
Brave New World

Kazuo Ishiguro
The Remains of the Day

Ben Jonson
The Alchemist

James Joyce
Dubliners

John Keats
Selected Poems

Philip Larkin
The Whitsun Weddings and Selected Poems

Christopher Marlowe
Doctor Faustus
Edward II

Arthur Miller
Death of a Salesman

John Milton
Paradise Lost Books I & II

Toni Morrison
Beloved

George Orwell
Nineteen Eighty-Four

Sylvia Plath
Selected Poems

Alexander Pope
Rape of the Lock & Selected Poems

William Shakespeare
Antony and Cleopatra
As You Like It
Hamlet
Henry IV Part I
King Lear
Macbeth
Measure for Measure
The Merchant of Venice
A Midsummer Night's Dream
Much Ado About Nothing
Othello
Richard II
Richard III
Romeo and Juliet
The Taming of the Shrew
The Tempest
Twelfth Night
The Winter's Tale

George Bernard Shaw
Saint Joan

Mary Shelley
Frankenstein

Jonathan Swift
Gulliver's Travels and A Modest Proposal

Alfred Tennyson
Selected Poems

Virgil
The Aeneid

Alice Walker
The Color Purple

Oscar Wilde
The Importance of Being Earnest

Tennessee Williams
A Streetcar Named Desire
The Glass Menagerie

Jeanette Winterson
Oranges Are Not the Only Fruit

John Webster
The Duchess of Malfi

Virginia Woolf
To the Lighthouse

William Wordsworth
The Prelude and Selected Poems

W.B. Yeats
Selected Poems

Metaphysical Poets